The Preaching Church

The Preaching Church

The Poor as *Sacra Praedicatio*

VINCENT J. PASTRO

Foreword by María Teresa Montes Lara, OP

RESOURCE *Publications* • Eugene, Oregon

THE PREACHING CHURCH
The Poor as *Sacra Praedicatio*

Copyright © 2016 Vincent J. Pastro. All rights reserved. Except for brief quotations in critical publications or reviews, no part of this book may be reproduced in any manner without prior written permission from the publisher. Write: Permissions, Wipf and Stock Publishers, 199 W. 8th Ave., Suite 3, Eugene, OR 97401.

Resource Publications
An Imprint of Wipf and Stock Publishers
199 W. 8th Ave., Suite 3
Eugene, OR 97401

www.wipfandstock.com

PAPERBACK ISBN 13: 978-1-62032-782-1
HARDCOVER ISBN 13: 978-1-4982-8758-6

Manufactured in the U.S.A.   02/12/2016

In Memory of Mom, Dad, and Rosemarie

Contents

Foreword by María Teresa Montes Lara, OP • ix
Notandae • xi
Acknowledgements • xiii

Introduction: Preachers by Baptism • 1

Part One: In-Between • 9

Chapter 1
The Real and Discipline in the Holy Preaching • 11

Chapter 2
Action and Suffering in the Holy Preaching • 21

Chapter 3
Praedicatio Crucis • 31

Chapter 4
Jesus Christ the *Nepantla* of God • 36

Chapter 5
Sacramentum Mundi • 45

Chapter 6
Preaching as Dialogue • 51

Part Two: Within • 57

Chapter 7
Locus Theologicus: Paying Attention • 60

Chapter 8
The Holy Preaching: Who not How • 68

Chapter 9
The Our Father • 76

Chapter 10
The Holy Spirit: Voice of the Preaching Church • 87

Part Three: Among • 97

Chapter 11
The Preaching Mexican Immigrant Community
in the United States • 99

Chapter 12
The Poor Church as Preacher • 108

Chapter 13
The Church and the Holy Trinity • 118

Chapter 14
All Creation Groans: Preaching and the Community of
Life • 127

Conclusion: An "Ontonomy" of the Holy Preaching • 137

References Cited • 143
Name Index • 151
Subject Index • 155
Scripture Index • 163

Foreword

When we speak of the missionary work of the people, everything is *evoked* and *provoked* by the Holy Spirit. The poor people of God respond to the urgings of the Comforter. The mission of the Spirit is lived in the *pueblo*, and this is pleasing to the Holy One who inspires. Is that not the mission of the Spirit? Is this mission *our* mission? Have we received the words of the risen Jesus into *our* hearts as he tells the first disciples: "Go into all the world and proclaim the good news to the whole creation" (Mark 16:15)? This is the gospel for the poor, for those who place themselves in solidarity with the poor, and for a universe crying out to the Spirit of love in "sighs too deep for words" (Rom 8:26). The preaching Church of the poor speaks, listens, and loves, becoming the Holy Preaching. This is Vincent Pastro's proposal for gospel proclamation. There is a privileged place here for the poor. That is where the Spirit places the divine option; the preaching Church, as well, makes God's option the poor community's option.

If the Spirit of God dwells within us, it is the Spirit who inspires us to speak and live the word of God, to proclaim the gospel in the name of Jesus. If we let the Spirit work within us, we become subjects of the Word. This work is the interaction between the people of God and the preacher, so that the preacher finds the work of the Spirit in the community, and the community's life resounds in the words of the preacher. The community itself becomes the Holy Preaching, as my friend says. We need one another. But we must let the Spirit work. For centuries, our Church community has been listening, echoing, and verbalizing what the Spirit reveals in the "signs of the times," in God's *anawim*. The people of God together, in the name of God, reflecting under the holy tent of the Word of God, ruminating, sometimes on Sundays, sometimes during the week, always under the influence of the creative Spirit who makes us a *pueblo*, a community, a people.

I once met a priest in Mexico who was "in charge" of forty communities. It was impossible to visit all of them every Sunday. But the Spirit called the community *together*. When the people of each community met weekly, the Spirit was present among the *pueblo*. We must not damper what the Spirit begins in the holy community. These Mexican communities in the indigenous *campo* shared the life-giving Spirit moving freely among them: "the word of God is not chained" (2 Tim 2:9). The *pueblo*, through baptism, are anointed by the Spirit to proclaim, to live, and to preach the word of God.

What Vince Pastro is addressing is the life of the baptized people, subjects of the work of the Spirit. The "little ones," the poor, with or without formal academic background, have responded to the promptings of the Holy Spirit, sometimes with the priest in their midst, sometimes without, all times through the unpredictable ways of the Spirit. They are the Holy Preaching, the "preaching Church of the poor," in Pastro's words. That is the case of immigrant communities throughout the world and, likewise, the Mexican immigrant community in the United States. They are the sacramental presence of the poor One in our midst. The Spirit speaks through them and inhabits those who are in solidarity with them.

Is the Spirit of the living God dwelling within us? Again, it is the work of the Spirit that *evokes* and *provokes*. Can we stop the hurricane and the gentle breeze (1 Kgs 19:11–13)? We are witnesses to the divine grace, and "it is marvelous in our eyes" (Ps 118:23). The poor community of the baptized proclaims the Word. The Spirit speaks. The Holy Preaching is the holy work of the poor people of God. Is this not always the way of the Spirit who indwells?

María Teresa Montes Lara, OP
Berkeley, CA

Notandae

Scripture quotes are taken from the New Revised Standard Version, unless otherwise noted. Bonhoeffer quotes, unless otherwise noted, are from the recently translated complete English works edited by Fortress Press. In the footnotes, these are abbreviated "*DBWE*" followed by the volume and page number (the German edition is abbreviated "*DBW*"). Complete editorial information is found in the bibliography.

In quotations taken from older English sources that did not use inclusive language, I have assumed that the theologian in question would do so today; instead, then, of the traditional *sic*, I have added in parenthesis the lacking modifiers. The exception is Raimon Panikkar, who believes that the word for the generic "Man" in English (with a capital "M") is necessary to his cosmic theology, i.e., "Man" is "more than human."[1] I am not sure why the word "Humanity," explained and capitalized to distinguish it from "humanity," would not capture the same idea; but out of respect for one of the great theologians of our time, I have neither changed what was not his intention nor added *sic*.

The reader will note that I consistently use "Fathers and Mothers" when speaking of our theological ancestors of the first centuries, or simply "Patristics and Matristics." I believe as many that it is important to speak of our *Mothers* in the faith, for they are both unrecognized and many. It has been pointed out that women did not leave a "written record" of the faith (although St. Perpetua

---

1. Panikkar, *The Intra-Religious Dialogue*, xiii.

now is thought to have left writings from her time in prison). While it is true that we do not have many historical documents of the early faith left by women (was it because they were not written or are there other reasons?), many theologians (not only women!) are beginning to speak of the Mothers. A notable example is Jaroslav Pelikan, who lists St. Macrina the Younger, sister to St. Basil the Great and St. Gregory of Nyssa, as one of the Cappadocian Fathers and Mothers. Macrina actually said that when Basil came back from his studies in Athens, she had to teach him true theology! If Gregory of Nyssa's tribute to his sister in *The Life of Macrina* is any indication, she is most certainly a Mother of the Church! One can also speak of Sts. Thecla, Macrina the Elder, Catherine of Alexandria, Perpetua and Felicity, Melania of Egypt, Olympias, and many more. It is high time that theology and the pastoral life of the Church community recognize its debt to women.

Acknowledgements

A book is never the work of an isolated individual. It is forged in the fire of the community of life. Words proceeding from the individual pen (or more likely these days the word processor!) are mere letters, smudges of ink on paper or pixels on a computer screen. The phrase, so important to both essay and music, is lost in smudges, pixels, and notes. For words to come alive in a book, or notes in music, they must be fired in the crucible of community.

So it is with this book. These are not my words, but belong to the community of life lived over the course of many years—the family in which I was raised, the fellow students with whom I have learned, the communities that I have pastored over the years. These words also rely on many whom I have only met through *their* words, in books and essays. I am grateful to this community of life that has nurtured me from the beginning; but I would like to mention a few who have been especially instrumental to the theology of preaching that ever changes in my own being.

I am grateful to my family of origin, three of whom enjoy the fullness of life in that great Church gathering, with us, of the *sanctorum communio*, the communion of saints—my father Eugene, my mother Emily, and my sister Rosemarie. Without them, I would not have had the gift of life. They are part of what Raimon Panikkar calls "tempiternity"—*kairos* time, if you will, in which all creation participates. To those in this "tempiternity" who are, gratefully, still part of not only *kairos* but *kronos* time, I give thanks—my sisters Margaret, Mary Anne, Patricia, Teresa, and my brother David.

Friends and colleagues have been many throughout the years—from the Maryknoll Fathers, Brothers, Sisters, Associates, and Affiliates, to the people of Perú, to the Mexican immigrant community I have had the privilege of pastoring and befriending, to the Tacoma Dominican Sisters with whom I am presently associated. The presbyters in my life have also been many: first and foremost, presbyters from the Archdiocese of Seattle, my "canonical community," but also Dominicans from the Central Province of the United States, especially Gregory Heille, OP, Maryknollers such as Peter Ruggere, MM, and Jesuits from the Oregon-California province, most especially Paul Janowiak, SJ, who has strongly influenced my own theology of preaching; but also Eddie Fernandez, SJ, Hung Pham, SJ, Thomas Massaro, SJ, George Quickley, SJ, and the Jesuit community of Berkeley. I would like to thank Professor Tamara Williams of Pacific Lutheran University in Tacoma, who helped arrange complete library privileges there; and Professor Sharon Callahan of the Seattle University School of Theology and Ministry, who has been a long-time supportive colleague and friend. The Brazilian section of the International Bonhoeffer Society has been caring and helpful over the years, especially Professor Carlos Caldas and Rev. Luis Cumaru.

There are two presbyters who I would especially like to mention—Fr. John Heagle and Fr. José Marins. John, a long-time friend and mentor, introduced me to the works of Fr. Raimon Panikkar. There have been many, part of the "community of words," who I do not know and will never meet until all are finally gathered into the arms of our gracious God—Dietrich Bonhoeffer especially, but also Karl Rahner, SJ, Juan Luis Segundo, SJ, Karl Barth, Otto Semmelroth, SJ, Catherine Mowry LaCugna, Edward Schillebeeckx, OP, John Meyendorff, Paul Evdokimov; and, among those belonging to *kronos* time, Leonardo Boff, Sr. Ivone Gebara, and Fr. Victor Codina, SJ. But lately I have been "bowled over" by the writings and witness of Raimon Panikkar, whose broadness, openness, and depth of person are evident in every word. Thanks to John for the

Acknowledgements

years of mentoring and for opening the Panikkar world of "ontonomy" to my theology of preaching. Fr. José Marins—along with Sr. Teolide María Trevisan—has also been a long-time mentor and friend. "Theologian and mentor at large" for the base ecclesial communities throughout the world, "Marins," as he is affectionately known by the many whose lives he has touched, has shown me what the "preaching Church" of the poor is all about.

Finally, words cannot express my indebtedness to my lifelong friend and colleague, María Teresa Montes Lara, OP, the director of the *Instituto Hispano* at the Jesuit School of Theology in Berkeley. She has graciously agreed to write the Forward for this volume and has patiently waded through the many drafts of this book. That alone would qualify her for immediate sainthood! On a much deeper level, though, these words have been tumbled like polished rocks by the many years of our friendship and collaboration, which cannot be repaid or adequately thanked. It is best to be grateful for the grace.

Introduction
Preachers by Baptism

> But you are a chosen race, a royal priesthood, a holy nation, God's own people, in order that you may proclaim the mighty acts of him who called you out of darkness into his marvelous light . . .
>
> God waited patiently in the days of Noah, during the building of the ark, in which a few, that is, eight persons, were saved through water.
>
> And baptism, which this prefigured, now saves you—not as a removal of dirt from the body, but as an appeal to God for a good conscience, through the resurrection of Jesus Christ, who has gone into heaven and is at the right hand of God, with angels, authorities, and powers made subject to him (1 Pet 2:9, 3:20–22).

One of the most ancient Christian beliefs, rooted in First Peter, the Letter to the Hebrews, and Revelation, is that we are *priests by our baptism*. When the sacred waters are poured upon us in the name of the Father, and of the Son, and of the Holy Spirit, when we are immersed in the saving waters, we enter into a relationship with the Holy Trinity, the "perfect Community" in the words of Leonardo Boff. This Community invites *us* to be community—a community that lives the baptism commitment. Jesus the High Priest makes us *priests*—"They sing a new song: 'You are worthy to take the scroll and to open its seals, for you were slaughtered and by your blood you ransomed for God saints from every

The Preaching Church

tribe and language and people and nation; you have made them to be a kingdom and priests serving our God, and they will reign on earth'" (Rev 5:8–10). It is a *priestly* task to preach—for all of us, from "every tribe and language and people and nation." Preaching is intimately connected with baptism. It is not simply the result of ordination, but a consecration, a charism, of the baptized.[1]

It has rightly been pointed out that traditional preaching these days is in serious trouble. Perhaps there is no better indicator than the Sunday homily. I say this with the deepest admiration and the utmost respect for those brave ordained preachers, men and women, who, like me, "dare the impossible" every Sunday morning.[2] Observers have proclaimed the death knell of the Sunday preaching for centuries—and it has always been a clarion call (generally unheeded) for a renewal of the *Holy Preaching*. The Catholic Church, as a result of the groundbreaking reforms of the Second Vatican Council, began to speak of the "liturgical homily." The homily was meant to be more conversational, more biblical, and less doctrinaire than the sermon. But in many Catholic schools of theology and ministry, preaching ("homiletics"!) was given last place, and "homily" came to mean "the shorter, the better." "No less than five minutes, no more than seven" is still the golden rule in more than a few Catholic institutions, along with encouragement to tell "lots of stories"— too often the inappropriate emotional revealing of "personal experiences" from the life of the ordained preacher!

The Protestant community in the United States, more traditionally attached to the Word than Catholics, fared better, and, in the 1970s, '80s, and '90s, trail-blazed what has been called "The New Homiletic." Exemplary preachers such as Fred Craddock, Barbara Brown Taylor, David Buttrick, and Eugene Lowry began to be taught in (even!) some Catholic schools of theology and

---

1 The Orthodox Bishops of the Church in America have promulgated an "encyclical letter" on preaching. They have said that preaching, properly speaking, is a charism of the baptized. At the same time, they talk about the "ordained preacher," whose ministry "from the ambo" is "within the entire community of believers." See https://oca.org/holy-synod/encyclicals/on-preaching.

2. Taylor, *When God is Silent*, 86.

Introduction

ministry. The New Homiletic was a radical attempt at renewal and offered (and still offers) much for the Church community to reflect on—what does the Church *do*, theologically and pastorally, when the Church *preaches*? But the New Homiletic, too, has often concentrated on methodology, presentation, and rhetoric, to the detriment of the *Holy Preaching*.

Simply put, preaching is, sadly, either dealt with inadequately or completely overlooked by many in theology today. Even classic Latin American liberation theology, one of the most creative and life-giving theologies of the late twentieth century, did not fare well regarding the Holy Preaching. There is little reference to the preaching event in many of the classic works of the theology of liberation. But the praxis of preaching is given short shrift not just there, where the proclamation for justice is integral part of the good news; it is often an afterthought in North American Catholic schools of theology, something relegated to the professor who has an extra space in their schedule. I hope to invite academy and Church to a radical reevaluation of the importance of the Holy Preaching. Perhaps in so doing, we can begin to "do theology" around a *praxis* of preaching, for as Gustavo Gutiérrez says, "Theology is a critical reflection on praxis in the light of the Word of God."[3] He invites us, I believe, to make the Holy Preaching part of our integral identity as a Church community. In speaking about prophetic denunciation (an integral part of the Holy Preaching), Gutiérrez says the following about *announcing* the gospel:

> The denunciation, however, is achieved by confronting a given situation with the reality which is *announced*: the love of the Father which calls all . . . in Christ and through the action of the Spirit to union among themselves and communion with him. To announce the Gospel is to proclaim that the love of God is present in the historical becoming of (hu)mankind. It is to make known that there is no human act which cannot in the last instance be defined in relation to Christ. To preach the Good News is for the Church to be a sacrament of history, to

3. Gutiérrez, *Theology of Liberation*, 15.

fulfill its role as community—a sign of the convocation of all . . . by God. It is to announce the coming of the Kingdom. The Gospel message reveals, without any evasions, what is at the root of social injustice: the rupture of the brotherhood (and sisterhood) . . .[4]

Preaching is inseparable from the preaching Church of the poor, the people of God. I am convinced that it is high time seriously to reevaluate the Sunday morning sermon-homily, with a critical theological analysis of *preaching*—which, unlike the traditional Sunday sermon, is very much alive. This book is an attempt to look closely at the *theology* of preaching (integrally connected with *ecclesiology*) and will not offer a "how to" for the Sunday sermon-homily. Rather, I invite ordained preachers—and the people of God who preach by their baptism—to reflect on the question "who," not "how," in the preaching. The *Who* is the risen Jesus, whose presence is manifested by the breath of the Holy Spirit in the *preaching Church of the poor*—particularly, for my purposes, the migrant Mexican community with whom I have ministered for many years. Preaching is so much deeper than the few moments on Sunday mornings that we traditionally associate it with. It is a way of life, a praxis of discipleship, a sharing of the poor Church with the poor, an evangelization of the wealthy by the preaching poor. Much of the ecclesiological work done in classic liberation theology forms the starting point for these reflections on the preaching Church of the poor:

> [T]he work of liberation is initiated and guided by the Spirit, not by human agency or motivation . . . the People of God, a key concept of liberation theology in its discussion of the Church, is the human agency of such change: that is, change is brought about by the people, who *are* the church . . . the People of God are the sons and *daughters* of the Church, men and women equal . . . found especially among the poor and the oppressed . . . as the People of God, men and women cooperate with

---

4. Ibid., 268–69.

Introduction

God in the act of creation, giving birth to a new heaven and earth.[5]

The Fathers and Mothers of the first centuries call this creative cooperation "synergy." The synergy of God's holy poor with the work of God (José Marins quotes Chrysostom: "God does the work, we do the sweating"!) will be key to understanding the words that follow.

My title, *The Preaching Church*, shamelessly pilfers from several sources that have been an inspiration to me over the many years of preaching: first, and most especially, the *Church*. I am not speaking of the institutional Church, for, as Dietrich Bonhoeffer said, "The Church is not an institution but a Person."[6] The Church is the people of God, the body of Christ, and the creation of the Holy Spirit. For this essential notion of Church, I am deeply indebted to the Second Vatican Council, to Archbishop Raymond G. Hunthausen, who ordained me presbyter many years ago in the spirit of the council, and to Hans Küng, a *peritus* (still an active theologian!) at the Second Vatican Council who encouraged the council bishops to give more prominence to the *Holy Spirit* in the Church community. I am also deeply grateful for the witness of Pope Francis during these first years of his papacy. One of his favorite metaphors for the Church community is Vatican II's "People of God." But most especially, I thank the poor and the base ecclesial communities with whom I have been privileged to minister—from slum dwellers of the *pueblos jóvenes* outside Lima, Perú, to the Mexican immigrant community in the Archdiocese of Seattle.

Second, my title shows the deepest respect for a book I read some years ago: *The Preaching Word*, by Otto Semmelroth, SJ. I became acquainted with Semmelroth's book through Paul Janowiak, SJ, (who rightly feels that Semmelroth should be included with Rahner and Schillebeekcx in the twentieth century "greats"

---

5. Musto, *Liberation Theologies*, xxi.
6. See *DBWE* 1. I first read this phrase from *Sanctorum Communio* in Bonhoeffer years ago but have not been able to locate the page number. See also Green, *Bonhoeffer: A Theology of Sociality*, 154.

of Catholic theology). Semmelroth treats the preaching event as an *integral* part of the Sunday liturgy, not "added on" nor, less, a "bridge" between the Liturgy of the Word and the Liturgy of the Eucharist (a notion still all too popular in many Catholic homiletic circles). The Sunday liturgy in its *entirety* is the incarnational presence of Christ, "Word" (*Wort*) of God for the people and "Answer" (*Antwort*) of the people to God in the Eucharist. "Preaching" in Semmelroth is a participial adjective that is part of the Word— more verb than noun. I hope that the title *The Preaching Church* conveys, in Semmelroth's tradition, the same notion for the Church, the *Gemeinde* community (Dietrich Bonhoeffer), a living Person Who is the Preaching Community of the Poor.

Third, my title is a tribute to the *Sacra Praedicatio*, the "Holy Preaching"—the ancient name of the Dominican Order and the title of Paul Janowiak's groundbreaking book some years ago on the theology of preaching.[7] Janowiak introduces the term by reminding us of the Dominicans, the "Holy Preaching" (some Dominican confreres say "Sacred Preaching" is a better translation), as St. Dominic of Guzman referred to the first members (women ten years before the men!) of his newly founded community of preachers. The phrase "Holy Preaching" stresses that "preaching," unlike "sermon" or "homily," is not properly a noun. It is a *verbal* activity.

Of the twentieth century European theologians, though, it is, in my opinion, Dietrich Bonhoeffer who has the most "living" notion of what preaching is about. It is, he says, the living Christ walking among the people:

> *The sermon derives from the incarnation of Jesus Christ and is determined by the incarnation of Jesus Christ . . .* The word of the sermon is the incarnate Christ. The incarnate Christ is God. Hence, the sermon is actually Christ. God *as* human being. Christ *as* the word. As the Word, Christ walks through the church-community.[8]

---

7. See Janowiak, *The Holy Preaching*.
8. *DBWE* 14:509–10.

Introduction

The people of God themselves, as the body of Christ quickened by the Holy Spirit, are the presence of the risen Jesus. I have, the last several years, been asking myself: is the living Christ walking among the people in the preaching event, the Christ that is the presence of the risen Jesus in the people? Yes, of course! But if that is true, do not the people of God have such an important role in the preaching that they themselves *become* the proclaiming presence of Christ, the "preaching Church"—a "transverbation," so to speak, of the Word and the people into Jesus Christ?[9] I firmly believe that this is so. Clyde E. Fant says that preaching occurs in the "midpoint" between the actual sermon-homily and the people. That midpoint, he says, is Jesus Christ.[10] I especially see in this "mid-point" the presence of the risen One *in the community*, in dialogue and unity with the world God has created. This *community* is the preaching Church.

Preaching is deeply contemplative and mystical. We have too easily forgotten that in the first centuries, the great mystics and pastors—Sts. Gregory of Nyssa, Macrina the Younger, Ephrem the Syrian, John Chrysostom, Catherine of Alexandria—were also the great preachers and theologians. There is an entire side of our tradition that says that God is mystery, *totaliter aliter* (Karl Barth), enveloped in darkness and "incomprehensibility" (St. Gregory of Nyssa). God is hidden in the darkness, *Deus Absconditus, Deus Crucifixus*. The great mystics wrote that God is found, if God is "found" at all, in the darkness, in the "cloud of unknowing." The "journey of the soul," as Saint John XXIII called it, is often not so much a movement from darkness into light, but from light into darkness, hiddenness, and the great mystery of the suffering of the poor and the world created by the God of life.

Fear of darkness permeates our being, perhaps, most especially, our preaching. What would happen if preaching led God's holy people on a journey not into "light" but into deeper darkness? What if preaching were *praedicatio abscondito, praedicatio crucis—sacra praedicatio*, a poor preaching Church of the poor,

---

9. Pastro, *Enflamed by the Sacramental Word*, 72–75.
10. Telephone interview, April 2012.

to paraphrase Pope Francis? The crucified poor preach the gospel, inviting us, through their imagination, into the darkness where the brilliance of the Holy Light of the Transfigured One is contemplated.

The Holy Preaching has little to do with the construction of words, or rhetorical structure, or use of language. It is much more—simple conversation, often "wordless," of the Holy Trinity with *us*.[11] It concerns Word, not words, Spirit, not rhetoric, and People, not "preacher." This book, then, presents a "big order": a critical, ecclesial, and theological questioning of our traditional notions of preaching that places the onus on the question "*Who*"? *Who* do we preach? *Who* is the Holy Preaching? *Who* is the preaching Church of the poor?

Vincent J. Pastro
Feast of the Transfiguration
August 6, 2015

---

11. The Fathers and Mothers call theology "the contemplation of the Holy Trinity."

Part One

IN-BETWEEN

> Theology is . . . a hazardous business, because the theologian establishes himself (herself) completely in the reality of revelation with the whole of his (her) human spirit and thinking mind. Theology is faith itself, alive in a thinking spirit. This thinking on the part of the human spirit is never finished. . . . But this emphasis on the use of philosophy in theology is inevitably accompanied by the danger of one-sidedness, the danger . . . that the aspect of mystery . . . may be forgotten. The contrary, however, is also true. In stressing this aspect of mystery and the saving significance of the reality of revelation, many modern theological movements also pay insufficient attention to the necessity of the *determinatio fidei*, the accurate definition of what enables the content of faith to be intelligibly understood within the mystery. This results in dogma becoming less clearly defined, and there is a serious threat that it may become emptied of content, or at least rootless.[1]

Edward Schillebeeckx's observation, written over sixty years ago, is even more valid today. Theology *is* a "hazardous business." The use of theological *ratio* these days—and *ratio* itself—is suspect. Is theology even a valid endeavor, when all things "religious" are,

1. Schillebeeckx, *The Schillebeeckx Reader*, 89–90.

Part One: In-Between

along with many academic disciplines, subject to the "hermeneutic of suspicion"? Perhaps preaching is presently among the *ratio* disciplines most highly suspect. So to take "churchy" endeavors like preaching and theology and place them under the microscope of analysis seems foolhardy at best! A "new paradigm" for preaching is necessary—and, like Schillebeeckx's theological *ratio*, a very "hazardous business." This "new paradigm" combines the *ratio* of the theology of preaching with experience of the poor in the twenty-first century, while respecting the Great Mystery that is the Triune God. For, after all, is not theology the "contemplation of the Holy Trinity," as the Fathers and Mothers would have it? The Holy Trinity desires nothing more than to "self-communicate," in the words of the great Karl Rahner, with the *pueblo* deeply loved.[2] The auto-communication of God regarding the Holy Preaching must theologically, within the divine mystery, account for the concrete Word-sacrament and its presence within the *pueblo*, the preaching Church community of the poor; it must be a healthy, non-oppressive, realistic preaching of the cross today; it asks the question "who" and not "how" regarding the Holy Preaching; it contemplates the Holy Trinity by looking at its "icon," the Church community; it looks for the presence of the Word in the *pueblo*; and it is, finally, attentive to the Spirit of Mystery. This kind of theology finds itself "in-between." Its task is two-fold: to avoid the "daunting dualisms" so prevalent in traditional theological *ratio*, and to "ratify the Real." Dietrich Bonhoeffer can be called the "theologian of the Real." What better way to begin a theology of preaching for the twenty-first century, where the priority is the poor preaching Church of the *Sacra Praedicatio*?

---

2. Rahner, *Foundations of the Christian Faith*, 116–37. The word *pueblo*—not used as such by Rahner—is a Spanish word used extensively in Latin American theology. It is really not translatable, but "poor people" would be a good English equivalent.

Chapter 1

The Real and Discipline in the Holy Preaching

It is absolutely astounding, I believe, that so much has been written in the last fifty years about the theology of Dietrich Bonhoeffer and, yet, so little about his theology of *preaching*.[1] Though preaching is often referred to in works about Bonhoeffer, and there has been fine work done on Bonhoeffer's theology of the word,[2] the fact remains that there is little that deals directly with what the pastor does on every Sunday of the year—*preach*. More importantly, very few have looked closely at Bonhoeffer's theology of preaching regarding the presence of Christ in the community—the community as the Holy Preaching. Preaching is important in Bonhoeffer *precisely* because of the historical context in the Germany of the Nazi era, in which he theologically looks closely at the *victim*.

The preaching ministry was deeply important to Bonhoeffer. Many sermon texts, like the Fathers and Mothers, form part of his theological corpus. We are also aware that Bonhoeffer moved in his theology from the academic chair to the ambo (it has been

---

1. Fant made this observation almost forty years ago. See *Bonhoeffer: Worldly Preaching*, ix—xi.
2. See, for instance, De Lange, *Waiting for the Word*.

Part One: In-Between

suggested that the ambo—the pulpit—is the academic chair of the preacher; Anna Carter Florence says that the preacher is the "resident theologian" of the community),[3] and from the ambo to the "world." There is no Bonhoeffer scholar who would not say that preaching held a central place in the activity of Bonhoeffer the theologian. But the only concerted effort I am aware of dealing directly with Bonhoeffer's theology and ministry of preaching in the English-speaking world is Clyde E. Fant's *Worldly Preaching*. Fant's book is an exegesis of Bonhoeffer's theology of preaching and, most especially, a commentary on, and translation of, the Finkenwalde lectures on preaching compiled from student notes. Bonhoeffer scholarship owes a largely unrecognized debt to Dr. Fant.[4]

My hope is to address the question of Bonhoeffer and the Holy Preaching in the first two chapters of this book—though perhaps in an untraditional way—by looking at a *contextual* reading of Bonhoeffer's theology of preaching. I will suggest something Bonhoeffer may not have considered when thinking about "the preacher" and preaching—although it is certainly present in his theology and life. This "implicit theology of preaching," fostered by 1) his Christological ecclesiology (the phrase is Eberhard Bethge's) and 2) the centrality of preaching in Bonhoeffer, will be the primary focus here: the *Gemeinde*-Church community as "preacher," the capacity of the *pueblo* to preach. Preaching is a charism of baptism, and ordination builds on baptism; but even in the sacramental traditions, the sacraments have their foundation in baptism and Eucharist.[5]

As theologians tell us, the Church community is the people of God, the body of Christ, and the creation of the Holy Spirit (Vatican II, Hans Küng). In Latin American theology, the word *pueblo*

---

3. See *Preaching as Testimony*.

4. It should be noted that the Finkenwalde Lectures on Preaching have been recently translated and published in *DBWE* 14:487–536 (2013). I use both Fant's and the Fortress translation of the lectures.

5. See Wingren, *The Living Word*, 104–107, for a classic Lutheran description of the doctrine of the priesthood of all believers through baptism.

The Real and Discipline in the Holy Preaching

is directed toward the community and the poor. How is the *pueblo*—specifically, the Mexican immigrant Church community in the United States—"the preacher"? How is the *pueblo* the preaching?

Bonhoeffer scholars have dealt extensively with the Christological ecclesiology that many consider the focal point of his theology. It revolves around what has become a catch phrase in Bonhoeffer studies: the Church is "Christ existing as Church community" (*Christus als Gemeinde existierend*).[6] This phrase, specifically used in *Sanctorum Communio*, is implicit in all of his later writings—including the *Letters and Papers*. Bonhoeffer held to this strong identification of Christ and the Church community despite opposition from theological colleagues. The Church community is *Gestalt Christi*,[7] the form of Christ, the *Christus praesens* (De Lange), Christ existing as community.

Similar to Bonhoeffer's identification of Christ with the Church community, preaching and the *pueblo*, in Bonhoeffer's theology, form an inseparable unity. I am well aware that the virtual identification of the *pueblo* with preaching will perhaps raise eyebrows in the homiletic-theological academy and the institutional Church—but the thesis of this book *is* a theology of preaching centered in the *pueblo* of God. A long-time pastor, preacher, and theologian, I thought, would be a good sounding board, and there is nobody better than Clyde E. Fant—no one is more knowledgeable about Bonhoeffer's theology of *preaching*, in my opinion. He confirmed my "suspicion." It is not off the mark, theologically, to talk about the *pueblo* and preaching in one breath. Fant maintains that there is a meeting point, a "midpoint," between the community of believers who are "listening" to a homily and the preacher himself or herself. That meeting point is where the preaching *occurs*. It is generally not something that can be pinned down to a specific event, a specific time or space, a specific place in the history of the Church community. The midpoint is Jesus Christ, says Fant.[8] For

---

6. *DBWE* 1:121

7. I became aware of the importance of this phrase while reading John W. de Gruchy. Unfortunately, I long ago forget the reference.

8. Telephone conversation, April 23, 2012.

Part One: In-Between

Bonhoeffer, the Church is "Christ existing as Church community," the *Gestalt Christi*, the *Christus praesens*, the living Christ walking, moving, breathing, among the people. It is at this midpoint where the *real* preaching happens.

As Bonhoeffer identifies the presence of Christ with the Church community, so it is, for Bonhoeffer, with the community and preaching. Preaching is the living Christ walking among the *pueblo*:

> The proclaimed Word is the incarnate Christ himself ... the preached Christ is the historical and the present Christ... He is the entrance to the historical Jesus. Therefore the proclaimed Word is not a medium of expression for something else, something which lies behind it, but it is the Christ himself walking through his congregation as the Word.[9]

Preaching is deeply connected with the incarnation of Jesus Christ. "Incarnational preaching" (the phrase is Fant's) is ecclesial, intricately connected with the people of God, the body of Christ, and the creation of the Holy Spirit—the *pueblo* as preaching Church community:

> The congregation is already present in the Embodied Christ; his body is "we ourselves." The church is included in the incarnation as the *sanctorum communio* . . . The proclaimed word is the Christ bearing human nature. This word is no new incarnation, but the Incarnate One who bears the sins of the world. Through the Holy Spirit this word becomes the actualization of his acceptance and sustenance. The word of the sermon intends to accept (hu)mankind, nothing else. It wants to bear the whole of human nature. In the congregation all sins should be cast upon the Word. Preaching must be so done that the hearer places all his (or her) needs, cares, fears, and sins upon the Word. The Word accepts all these things. When preaching is done in this way, it is the proclamation of Christ . . . The Word is there that burdens might be laid

---

9. Bonhoeffer quoted by Fant, *Preaching for Today*, 43. Also *Worldly Preaching*, 126.

The Real and Discipline in the Holy Preaching

upon it. We are all borne up by the word of Christ. Because it does so, it creates fellowship. Because the Word includes us into itself, it makes us members of the body of Christ. As such we share in the responsibility of upholding one another . . . The Word intends that no one should remain alone, for in him no one remains alone. The Word makes individuals part of one body. . . [The Word] seeks community, it needs community, because it is already laden with humanity.[10]

The people *and* the preaching are the *Christus praesens*. We can say, then, that the people—the *pueblo*—are "the Holy Preaching."[11] The poor, in their preaching, are *Gestalt Christi*. The Church of the poor is the concrete *Gestalt Christi*, and *their preaching* becomes *Gestalt Christi*. Bonhoeffer says that preaching is integral part of the identity of the Church community. The preacher himself or herself is not really the "preacher"; rather it is the Word that forms the preaching deep in the heart of the *pueblo*:

> The preacher does not therefore accomplish the application of the word; he (or she) is not the one who shapes it and forms it to suit the congregation. With the introduction of the biblical word the text begins moving among the congregation. Likewise the word arises out of the Bible, takes shape as the sermon, and enters into the congregation in order to bear it up.[12]

I believe that a contextual reading of Bonhoeffer within situations of oppression and poverty, and specifically with the Mexican

---

10. Fant, *Worldly Preaching*, 127.

11. The "Holy Preaching," or perhaps as Dominican scholars will say the "Sacred Preaching" (*sacra praedicatio*), is the name St. Dominic of Guzman gave to his newly founded community of preachers in the twelfth century. Dominican theology, including Thomas Aquinas, Bartolomé de Las Casas, Edward Schillebeeckx, Mary Catherine Hilkert, and Gustavo Gutiérrez, is centered in the "Holy Preaching"—the community of believers *and* the preaching event. Latin American theologians speak of two primary *loci theologici*—the Church and the poor (Gustavo Gutiérrez, José Marins). The *pueblo* and ecclesial preaching are, by extension, important *loci theologici* in Latin America and in the Mexican immigrant community in the United States.

12. *Worldly Preaching*, 128.

Part One: In-Between

immigrant Church in the United States, will "prove the axiom." I will approach the question by using Bonhoeffer's prison poem *Stations on the Way to Freedom* as concrete manifestation of the preaching of the poor Church as *Gestalt Christi*. It is a brief poem full of simplicity and depth, revolving around four "stations": discipline, action, suffering, and death, perhaps reflecting, in Bonhoeffer's mind, the Catholic devotion of the Stations of the Cross. The reader can readily reference the poem on the Internet or textually in the Fortress *Dietrich Bonhoeffer Works*.[13]

Discipline: Preaching as Disciplina Arcani

The first station is *discipline*. Did Bonhoeffer have the *disciplina arcani* in mind?[14] No doubt Dietrich Bonhoeffer was "disciplined" in the way he lived. From his study of music to theology, from his professorships to his pastorates, from his careful selection of words to his participation in the plot against Hitler, he led a "disciplined" life. For Bonhoeffer, discipleship is a discipline, a *theologia crucis*. The way of discipline is the way of the cross. Discipline, for Bonhoeffer, is not a "denial of self" for the sake of "spiritual strength." The journey toward the cross, very simply, requires *discipline*.

The *disciplina arcani* was a practice of the early Church during periods of persecution and martyrdom.[15] It was a favorite theme of Bonhoeffer. The idea was a careful "guarding" of the "sacred mysteries" of the faith from profanation. What was considered sacred was not to be thrown to the dogs (Matt 7:6, 15:26, Mark 7:27). This was not simply out of respect; it was primarily, I believe, for the *safety* of the community. Martyrdom was never sought for martyrdom's sake. It was, rather, a *consequence* of faithful discipleship.

---

13. See *DBWE* 8:512–514.

14. This Latin phrase is often translated "secret discipline" and refers to the practice in the early Church of the careful guarding of the sacred mysteries, the sacraments. I prefer the translation "hidden discipline."

15. The Fortress Press editors of the *Letters and Papers* discuss the translation of the phrase and decided upon "arcane discipline" to avoid the word "secret" with its Gnostic overtones. See *DBWE* 8:32.

The Real and Discipline in the Holy Preaching

Specifically, the *disciplina arcani* was practiced by the early Church in the strict "guarding" of the sacraments—the "mysteries"—from profanation by the Roman Empire. No one was admitted to the Eucharist without first passing through a strict, disciplined, lengthy process of catechumenate. What the early Church perhaps had in mind was the strict guarding of the *community*, the *Sacrament of Christ* (E. Schillebeeckx), from the profanation of martyrdom. What was guarded here was *life*—the life in abundance that is the most precious gift, in Jesus and the Spirit, of the living God.

Bonhoeffer specifically refers to the *disciplina arcani* in the *Letters and Papers* (*DBWE* 8). But it is implicit throughout all of his theology.[16] His reflections on silence and preaching are, perhaps, a reference to preaching as *disciplina arcani*. In his baptismal sermon sent from prison for his godchild Dietrich, the son of Eberhard Bethge and his niece Renate, Bonhoeffer (as in *Discipleship*, *DBWE* 4) reflects on how words, like grace, are "cheap" for the Church.[17] The Church is too careless with the words of faith—especially in preaching—and uses them frivolously. This forms the basis for his criticism of Karl Barth in the *Letters and Papers*, the famous "positivism of revelation" charge.[18] In a direct use of the phrase *disciplina arcani* (*Arkandisziplin*), he asks in this baptismal sermon:

> What does a church, a congregation, a sermon, a liturgy, a Christian life, mean in a religionless world? How do we talk about God—without religion, that is, without the temporally conditioned presuppositions of metaphysics, the inner life, and so on? How do we speak (or perhaps we can no longer even "speak" the way we used to) in a "worldly" way about God? How can we go about being "religionless-worldly" Christians, how can we be

---

16. As, for instance, in *Discipleship*. The editors of *DBWE* 8 say that references are found in *Discipleship* without specific use of *Arkandisziplin*. See *DBWE* 4:45, footnote 11, and *DBWE* 4:53–54, footnote 36, where the editors mention that Bonhoeffer talked "extensively" about the ancient Church and the *disciplina arcani* at Finkenwalde in the context of Nazi Germany.

17. *DBWE* 8:383–90.

18. Ibid., 364, 373.

Part One: In-Between

ek-klesia, those who are called out, without understanding ourselves religiously as privileged, but instead seeing ourselves as belonging wholly to the world? Christ would no longer then be the object of religion, but something else entirely, truly Lord of the world. But what does that mean? In a religionless situation, what do ritual and prayer mean? Is this where the "arcane discipline," or the difference (which you've heard about from me before) between the penultimate and the ultimate, have new significance?[19]

The Holy Preaching is *disciplina arcani*. It is directed toward the protection of life. It *is* a discipline, as every preacher knows. Prayer, study, and preaching are disciplined work. John Holbert maintains that preaching, as a discipline, is physically demanding. The preacher should care for the self. Eating correctly, exercising regularly, and getting enough sleep are as important as study and prayer in the life of the preacher.[20] The *disciplina arcani* is an exigency placed upon the Holy Preaching, whether ordained preacher or poor preaching community.

The *disciplina arcani* of preaching consoles; but it also *confronts*. It is a discipline for the preacher or for the *pueblo*, the *Gestalt Christi* who preaches, to discern which: *consolation* of the suffering poor or *confrontation* of the dominant community. The integral connection of announcing and denouncing is always part of the Holy Preaching. Preaching is a *disciplina arcani*, a careful guarding of the gift of life against profanation. Preaching must always be centered in life as we live it *here and now*—as Bonhoeffer said, the concern for what is concrete and real.[21] The promise of Jesus is life; and life in Christ begins *now*.

On May 1, 2008, the immigrant community—largely Mexican and undocumented—gathered in the cities of the United States to manifest their demand for a life of human dignity, unhampered by immigration raids, underemployment, and the poverty of being

19. Ibid., 364–65.

20. Holbert, *Preaching Creation*, 108.

21. DBWE 6:47–49, 76–77, 262–270. Reality has no existence and is only an "abstraction" outside of the "Real One," Jesus Christ.

The Real and Discipline in the Holy Preaching

"without papers." Perhaps fifty thousand people marched through downtown Seattle alone. They were Mexican, but joined by other Latinos(as), Asian people, African-Americans, people from the dominant culture, middle class workers, Church communities, IBEW representatives, Teamsters, and many others. They gathered to demand long overdue immigration reform. An older Mexican man carried a sign that read: "I am not illegal. I am a human being." "The thief comes only to steal and kill and destroy," says Jesus. "I came that they may have life, and have it abundantly" (John 10:10). The base ecclesial communities of Holy Spirit Parish in Kent, WA, were among the marchers. People have gathered every May 1 since to continue this *disciplina* (perhaps not so *arcani!*) where life is cared for and respected. The marchers, as Bonhoeffer relates in his poem, "set out to seek freedom" in discipline. "*Only through discipline does one learn the secret of freedom,*" Bonhoeffer proclaims in the poem. The Church *en marcha*, the *pueblo de Dios*, the *Gestalt Christi*, preached eloquently. The formal event of the Sunday preaching, in dialogue with the *pueblo*, meets at the "midpoint" (Fant) that is Jesus Christ. The midpoint is often disciplined action such as the Worker's Day immigration rights marches.

The Mexican immigration situation grows ever more unjust—perhaps one of the gravest ethical issues confronting the United States. Some recent statistics indicate that Mexican immigration in the United States is presently down.[22] However, xenophobia and racism among the dominant community continues and is not the exception but the rule. In the last few years, Arizona and Alabama have passed stringent anti-immigrant laws. Their enforcement has been delayed because of challenges by Churches and immigration rights groups, the federal government, and others. It is not without reason that Pope Francis has chosen the immigrant as one of the focal points of his papacy. He has said specifically that he is watching the border between Mexico and the United States.

---

22. Pew Research Center, April 2012. See http://pewresearch.org/pubs/2250/mexican-immigration-immigrants-illegal-border-enforcement-deportations-migration-flows.

Part One: In-Between

Discipline is an important aspect in Bonhoeffer's theology of preaching and occupies an important place poetically expressed in the *Stations on the Way to Freedom*. I will now look, in the following chapter, at action and suffering in the Holy Preaching.

Chapter 2

Action and Suffering in the Holy Preaching

Stellvertretung is an often-used word in the Bonhoeffer corpus, consistently translated as "vicarious representative action" in the Fortress *Dietrich Bonhoeffer Works*. Bonhoeffer uses it to describe what Jesus does *pro nobis*. Many say it can be used as a "summary word" for Bonhoeffer's theology.[1] He succinctly describes its Christological core. Note the connection with the Real and its identity with the person of Christ:

> Action in accord with Christ does not originate in some ethical principle, but in the very person of Jesus Christ. This is because everything real is summed up in Christ, who, by definition, is the origin of any and all action that is in accord with reality.
>
> Jesus Christ is the very embodiment of the person who lives responsibly. He is not the individual who seeks to attain his own ethical perfection. Instead, he lives only as the one who in himself has taken on and bears the selves of all human beings. His entire life, action, and suffering is vicarious representative action [*Stellvertretung*]. As the one who has become human he indeed stands in the place of all human beings. All that human beings

---

1. Tödt, *Authentic Faith*, 1–15, 62–63.

were supposed to live, do, and suffer falls on him. In this real vicarious representative action in which his human existence consists, he is the responsible human being par excellence. All human responsibility is rooted in the real vicarious representative action of Jesus Christ on behalf of all human beings. Responsible action is vicarious representative action. Vicarious representative action is not presumptuous and overbearing only insofar as it is grounded in God's becoming human, which brought about the real vicarious representative action of Jesus Christ on behalf of all human beings. It is only on this ground that there is genuine vicarious representative action and thus responsible action.[2]

"Seek the right thing... boldly reach for the real... Dare to quit anxious faltering and enter the storm of events," says Bonhoeffer in the poem *Stations on the Way to Freedom*. Preaching is the "action" of Christ. Reflecting on sermons he preached as a young man in Barcelona, Bonhoeffer writes how he had previously believed that a sermon always had to have a "central point." In Finkenwalde, he comes to believe that there is really no central point to preaching— it "apprehends" nothing. Rather, preaching is only "apprehended by" Jesus Christ.[3] It is not about "the preacher": "For I decided to know nothing among you except Jesus Christ, and him crucified" (1 Cor 2:2). Because the *pueblo* is the form of Christ and preaching is "apprehended by" Jesus, the preaching itself becomes the *Gestalt Christi* in the people.

On December 21, 1511, on the Caribbean island of *Quisquella* (renamed *La Española* by the colonists and now present-day Dominican Republic and Haiti), Dominican Friar Antonio de Montesinos stepped into the pulpit of the church of Santo Domingo and preached one of the most famous social justice homilies ever delivered. Though not well-known outside Latin America, it is a denunciation against the genocide of the enslaved indigenous *Taíno* who toiled in the Spanish gold mines. Montesinos' text was John 1:23— "[John the Baptist] said, 'I am the voice of one crying

2. *DBWE* 6:231–32.
3. Fant, *Worldly Preaching*, 12.

Action and Suffering in the Holy Preaching

out in the wilderness, Make straight the way of the Lord,' as the prophet Isaiah said." Friar Antonio, though, did not preach as the Baptist. He was "the voice of *Christ* crying in the wilderness of this island."[4] When the government authorities went to the priory after the preaching demanding Montesinos, Pedro de Córdoba, the superior, told Diego de Colon, the governor and the son of Christopher Columbus, that the Spanish colonists would have to detain *all* the friars. *All* had *communally* prepared the "Holy Preaching." All preached with Montesinos that day—each and every friar of the community signed the text. When Montesinos said that he was "the voice of Christ," the entire Dominican community was in the pulpit—*Gestalt Christi, Christus praesens*, the Holy Preaching, the "living Christ walking among the people."[5]

These courageous friars provide a model for what the Holy Preaching is at core—a community, gathered by the Spirit in the name of Jesus, to *be* the voice of Christ in the wilderness. A large part of "faith formation" (Bonhoeffer prefers the word *conformitas*) that should occur in communities of Mexican immigrants, in my opinion, is preparation of the *pueblo* to let Christ "take form" in them by the breath of the Spirit—*Gestalt Christi*. Formal preaching, liturgy, and adult formation are united into one action, as it were, an *epiclesis*—a calling down of the Holy Spirit upon the sacramental gifts that are the *pueblo*—Augustine of Hippo's "become what you receive."[6] The *pueblo* is prepared as "preacher." José Marins, Gonzalo Ituarte, Ernesto Cardenal, and others propose a communal approach in which the people actually "do" the preaching through discussion of the Sunday scriptural texts.[7] The *pueblo*

---

4. Two short paragraphs, written twenty years after the preaching, are all that we have left of the text of this famous preaching. See De Las Casas, *The History of the Indies*, 183–84.

5. See the discussion of the Montesinos preaching in Pastro, *Enflamed by the Sacramental Word*, 18–21.

6. Augustine, Sermon 272, http://www.earlychurchtexts.com/public/augustine_sermon_272_eucharist.htm.

7. See Cardenal, *The Gospel in Solentiname*. José Marins refers to this methodology as "chit-chat," where the formal preacher asks the people to discuss in twos a question related to the Sunday readings. Gonzalo Ituarte,

preach, and the "preacher" coordinates the discussion in what becomes the formal act of preaching. Alternatively, one of the leaders in the CEBs (base ecclesial communities) is invited to preach; afterwards, the people actively participate through a discussion of the scriptural themes.

Stellvertretung is "vicarious representative action." It is what Jesus does for the people. But the people themselves are *Gestalt Christi* for Bonhoeffer. The people, as Church community, people of God, body of Christ, and creation of the Holy Spirit, become the "form" of Christ. Jesus "takes form" in the *pueblo*. Karl Barth says the preacher is *vicarius Christi*.[8] If it is the people in the form of Christ who preach, then it is the *pueblo*, in its preaching, that is *vicarius Christi* in the *action* of preaching and in their *action* as disciples of Christ day by day. Bonhoeffer anticipates this Latin American model in the following prophetic words spoken in 1935:

> The pastor, and particularly the young pastor, suffers from being by himself (herself). The burden of preaching is particularly heavy today for the solitary pastor who is not a prophet, but just a servant of the church. He needs brotherly help and fellowship not only to show him what he is to preach, but also to show him how to preach it. . . . Preaching which has its roots in practical work, as well as *in the life and the experience of the community*, will be more relevant, and less likely to run the risk of either being intimidated or bogged down.[9]

He is, of course, talking about the "preacher" in the traditional sense. But the community is primary. The *pueblo*, in their preaching, is *Stellvertretung*—the "vicarious representative action" of Christ. Like Antonio de Montesinos, the people are the *voice of Christ* in their preaching. Bonhoeffer would concur: "[N]othing,

---

OP, (interviewed in June 2005 at the Dominican house in Mexico City) uses a similar methodology with indigenous Mexican communities in Chiapas.

8. Barth, *Homiletics*, 57.

9. Fant, *Worldly Preaching*,18, italics mine.

Action and Suffering in the Holy Preaching

(Bonhoeffer) insisted, is more concrete than the real voice of Christ speaking in the sermon."[10]

Suffering: Preaching as the Form of Christ

"Wondrous transformation . . . Yet now you breathe a sigh of relief and lay what is righteous calmly and fearlessly into a mightier hand," says Bonhoeffer in *Stations*. In the classic understanding of *conformitas*, we "conform" ourselves to Christ. We "imitate" Christ, as St. Thomas à Kempis says. Bonhoeffer gives new meaning to *conformitas*—it is, rather, Jesus Christ, by the work of the Holy Spirit, who *conforms himself to us*.[11] Note the strong connection between the person of Christ, action, the community, and proclamation:

> Ethics as formation, then, is the venture of speaking about the form of Christ taking form in our world neither abstractly nor casuistically, neither programmatically nor purely reflectively. Here we must risk making concrete judgments and decisions. Here decision and deed can no longer be shifted onto the individual's personal conscience. Here concrete commandments and guidance are given, for which obedience will be demanded. Ethics as formation is possible only on the basis of the form of Jesus Christ present in Christ's church. *The church is the place where Jesus Christ's taking form is proclaimed and where it happens.* The Christian ethic stands in the service of this proclamation and this event.[12]

Bonhoeffer describes how *conformitas* is a discernment of the will of God. It can only happen on the basis of a radical transformation, a conversion of the heart and mind, so that the mind and heart is *Christ's* mind and heart:

> Now how does this discernment of "what is the will of God" take place? Here, the decisive and clear prerequisite

10. Ibid., 19, quote from E. Bethge.
11. *DBWE* 6:76–102.
12. *DBWE* 6:102.

is that such discernment can take place only on the basis of a "metamorphosis," a complete inner change of the existing form, a "renewal" of the mind (Rom 12:2), to living as children of the light (Eph 5:9). This "metamorphosis" of human beings can only mean overcoming the form of the fallen human being, Adam, and con-formation [*Gleichgestaltung*] with the form of the new human being, Christ.[13]

Jesus takes form in the people through the action of the Holy Spirit. *Conformitas* is cruciform. It involves the mystery of the liberating cross of the Crucified One who is risen from the dead (Louis-Marie Chauvet).

"In this you rejoice, even if now for a little while you have had to suffer various trials, so that the genuineness of your faith—being more precious than gold that, though perishable, is tested by fire—may be found to result in praise and glory and honor when Jesus Christ is revealed" (1 Pet 1:6–7). Suffering, for Bonhoeffer, is not something "sought out"—the follower of Jesus never *looks* for martyrdom, but life is protected (*disciplina arcani*) at all costs. The traditional view of suffering in the Christian life *demands* radical reevaluation so that emotionally unhealthy traits of suffering, cross, and death are addressed at root. For too long, the poor have been told to fix their eyes on the "here after" and to "accept" suffering from the hand of God. Marx's critique of religion (very close, in fact, to Bonhoeffer's) is correct: religion, in this light, *is* the "opium of the people." The poor are anesthetized with the "here after." This view of suffering is individualistic and unhealthy. When Bonhoeffer speaks of the suffering of the *Gestalt Christi*, he is, rather, pointing to the "wondrous transformation" of the *pueblo* that the cross and resurrection of Jesus effects.

In Bonhoeffer's *conformitas*, Christ takes form in the *pueblo* here and now. Suffering is transformed. Freedom is placed in God's hands so that it can be "perfected in glory." It is this "perfection in glory" that takes the eyes of the preaching *pueblo* off the "other world" and places them squarely on what they are suffering at the

---

13. Ibid., 322.

Action and Suffering in the Holy Preaching

hands of the oppressor. Through this transformation, the *pueblo* preach, with Christ, from the cross—the crucified people, says Jon Sobrino.[14] Suffering is not the "lot" of the poor; it is inflicted by the powerful. The cross is an "eloquent pulpit."[15]

I once buried a young Mexican man killed while working under hazardous conditions in an oyster processing plant. He was pinned by a forklift in a cooler, where he quickly experienced hypothermia when no one heard his cries for help. The work accepted by Mexican immigrants in the United States can be extremely dangerous—roofing without proper harnessing, construction work without proper training, or toxic decontamination without proper protection. Mexican workers in the United States readily accept dangerous labor no longer done by English-speaking people. If there were a general strike of Mexican workers in the United States, the country would grind to a halt—exactly what happened in Alabama some years ago with anti-immigrant legislation. Many Mexican immigrants simply left the state. The jobs they performed—in agriculture and the fishing industry—were left vacant. On the first Worker's Day manifestations throughout the country, people marched instead of going to work. If Bonhoeffer were writing about preaching in the context of the Mexican immigrant, he would consider this the preaching of the *pueblo* as *Gestalt Christi*, the prophetic voice of Christ crying for justice.

Death: Preaching as Theologia Crucis

The *fiesta*, the "feast," is deeply significant for the Mexican community—a celebration of life in the midst of the suffering *pueblo*. There is always time for *fiesta*, whether baptism, marriage, or funeral. The *fiesta* is life. Bonhoeffer says this last station is the "highest of feasts"—the way to "eternal freedom." He uses the first person plural in this last stanza because *theologia crucis* is communal. Like suffering, it can never be simply individual. *Theologia*

---

14. Sobrino, *Christology at the Crossroads*, 179–235.
15. Pastro, *Enflamed*, 84. I believe this is Jon Sobrino's phrase.

Part One: In-Between

crucis is a communal cross; it is the *pueblo* that bears the cross to Calvary.

Gregory Heille, OP, says that "all good Christian preaching leads to the foot of the cross." When it is the poor *pueblo* who preach, the entire community preaches from the cross, which, in turn, becomes the ambo, the "pulpit," of the *pueblo*.[16] Bonhoeffer calls the way of the cross the "highest of feasts," a station on the way to "eternal freedom" sharing the life and the freedom of the living God—the only freedom, for Bonhoeffer, which makes sense. Freedom is not so much, says Bonhoeffer, the freedom to "preach the gospel." It is, rather, the freedom of the Church community to be in solidarity with the victim.[17] The preaching Church becomes martyr, like Blessed Oscar Romero and Dietrich Bonhoeffer. Preaching was paramount to both; Archbishop Romero was martyred immediately after preaching, and Dietrich Bonhoeffer less than twenty-four hours after an Easter homily. Both were the *pueblo*: "If I am killed, I will rise again in the Salvadoran people," said Blessed Oscar.

In the vast and large desert that lies at the border between the United States and Mexico, many Mexicans have died trying to make their way into the United States. Official estimates are conservative. The numbers are surely higher:

> In October 1994, the Immigration and Naturalization Service (INS) launched Operation Gatekeeper to crack down on people entering the country through San Diego, California. Militarizing the border with more border patrol agents and resources has forced immigrants to cross through the Imperial Desert or over the mountains north of Tecate. Global Exchange states that the number of immigrant deaths has increased over 600 percent since 1994. Several thousands have died along the U.S./Mexico border since Operation Gatekeeper began. Mexicans have drowned in canals and rivers and have died of dehydration, hypothermia and heat stress in the desert.

---

16. The image is Jon Sobrino's

17. John W. de Gruchy in the Doblmeier film *Bonhoeffer: Pastor, Pacifist, Nazi Resister*.

Action and Suffering in the Holy Preaching

Some have been shot by ranchers in Arizona and Texas. In the year 2000 alone, 369 immigrants perished trying to cross the border—almost half from exposure to heat or cold. Because of increasing amounts of border patrol officers and equipment, many undocumented workers are staying longer in the U.S., unable to return to see their families for long periods of time and swelling the immigrant population.[18]

According to *Agence France-Presse*, in an article written in October of 2009, over six thousand Mexicans have died in the desert attempting to cross into the United States in the past fifteen years. The exact figures, cited by the American Civil Liberties Union and originating with the Mexican foreign ministry, are 6,607. United States Homeland Security says 3,861. That does not count the years between 2009 and the present.

The Mexican people in the United States, many who are undocumented with little hope of obtaining papers, have died numerous deaths—leaving family and home; crossing the desert border; lack of documentation; unemployment and underemployment; discrimination on the part of the dominant culture; lack of understanding from civil and ecclesial authorities; poverty; lack of medical insurance; few benefits at work; and many challenges besides. The Sunday border is an even greater challenge for the *pueblo* that is, in its majority, baptized Catholic. The people come to North American Catholic parishes where there is often good will but small concrete effort to accept the *pueblo* as common sojourners.

The crucified *pueblo* preach powerfully—and prophetically—from the pulpit of the cross. On the cross, they are the crucified, bloodied, wounded, dead Christ, as Bartolomé de Las Casas says, "Christ crucified not once but thousands of times."[19] The station of death is the last station on the way to "eternal freedom." "By his wounds we are healed" (Isa 53:4). In the death of the preaching *Gestalt Christi*, mysteriously hidden like the *Deus absconditus*, lies

18. http://www.pbs.org/itvs/beyondtheborder/immigration.html
19. See Gutiérrez, *En Busca de los Pobres de Jesucristo*.

the life of the risen One, the Holy Preaching living in the *pueblo*. But how is this salvific for the *pueblo*? How does the destructive image of cross, suffering, and death, used to control the poor for so many centuries, bring liberation, resurrection, life?

Chapter 3

Praedicatio Crucis

Dietrich Bonhoeffer's *Stations on the Road to Freedom* is a beautiful poem expressing his mystical experience in a Nazi prison—the experience of a committed man who knew the Nazis would execute him. It has eternal value and speaks to every context. But how is the *Sacra Praedicatio* in the poor preaching Church connected to the cross of Jesus *today*? Who is Jesus Christ for us *today*, as Bonhoeffer asked his students? How do we speak with the poor today about suffering, death, and the cross, central tenets of our faith so often abused and misused by the dominant community to keep the poor "in their place"? Or put another way, do the dominant *really* listen to the suffering of the poor?

It is absolutely necessary, then, to look closely at traditional theologies of the cross so that they do not become oppressive to the poor. Theologians and pastors must *listen* to the poor preaching Church. The Holy Preaching can no longer be "business as usual" with the accustomed speakers. This new preaching lets the poor *speak*. The poor become the Holy Preaching and the preaching Church, and the Church listens to the voice of the suffering poor. Perhaps Jon Sobrino, SJ, suggests the most important question: how do we take the poor from the cross?[1] Leonardo Boff, as well, addresses the root problem: how does the theology of the

1. See Sobrino, *The Principle of Mercy*.

cross move from traditional "satisfaction" or "atonement"—these are only *theories* about the cross—to the cross as direct consequence of the commitment of Jesus to the poor?[2] The Fathers and Mothers remind us that salvation is not just "the cross." The *Incarnation* too, in communion with the cross and resurrection, is salvific. Incarnation—the flesh, the human life of Jesus including his death—is what saves. "What was not assumed cannot be saved" is a Christological adage as traditional as the cross.

Second Isaiah says: "Get you up to a high mountain, O Zion, herald of good tidings; lift up your voice with strength, O Jerusalem, herald of good tidings, lift it up, do not fear; say to the cities of Judah, 'Here is your God'" (Isa 40:9). The preacher here is not the prophet; it is Zion and Jerusalem, a holy *community*, the *Sacra Praedicatio*. The preacher is also the "listener"—"the cities of Judah," the Holy People of God. Preacher and listener are not separated but caught up in the unity of the Holy Preaching. Second Isaiah's message is: "*Here* is your God!" The message of the Holy Preaching is founded upon that *here*. The Holy Preaching points to the presence of God here and now, in every context. For followers of Jesus, a mysterious and primal revelation of that presence is the cross of Jesus. *Who would ever look for God there*, in the *Deus Crucifixus*, the *Deus Absconditus*? This is precisely where the preaching Church squarely faces the question of the unjust suffering of the poor. The Holy Cross is where "all good Christian preaching leads," as Gregory Heille, OP, reminds us. The cross is the *consequence* of the commitment to the poor. It forms part and parcel of the *life*, the flesh, of the redeemed in Jesus. The cross is Hope Embodied. Jurgen Moltmann writes that when the Jesuit fathers and the two women were brutally murdered in El Salvador in November of 1989, a copy of *The Crucified God* had fallen into the blood of one of the martyred Jesuits. This senseless brutality gave ultimate meaning to the cross of Jesus, Moltmann felt.[3] The cross is the result of the commitment with the poor.

---

2. Boff, *Passion of Christ*.
3. Moltmann, *The Crucified God*, xi–xii.

Praedicatio Crucis

If we speak of a *theologia crucis*, we must also speak of a *praedicatio crucis*—but from the perspective of the poor. *Praedicatio crucis* is only done in solidarity with the poor. It cannot be done in safety: "If any want to become my follower, let them deny themselves and take up their cross and follow me" (Matt 16:24). "Taking up the cross" has often meant: "Bear your lot in life, that is your cross, that is what you must endure." The cross, then, becomes an instrument of torture. But to the contrary, the cross is the *injustice* from which the poor must be taken down, the consequence of a life of faithful discipleship: "Love your enemies" (Matt 5:44). It is the result of the Incarnation lived to the fullest, the face of the risen Jesus, a life offered in loving sacrifice for the other. Death and life, life and death, are of the same fabric, of one indivisible piece. Divide them and they no longer *are*, for the life in abundance promised by Jesus does not exist (John 10:10) without death and the cross.

What does *praedicatio crucis*, the preaching of the cross, do today, if traditional theologies of atonement, according to Sobrino and Boff, are in need of radical revision? It does two things: 1) it gives priority to solidarity with the poor, that is, to the commitment to remove the poor from the cross of oppression; and 2) it helps us to see the cross as consequence of committed discipleship, a life of following the Incarnate One through solidarity with the poor. Additionally Boff, along with many, reminds us that the universe created by God is oppressed with the poor. How do we respect the life incarnated by God in Jesus—the life of the poor *and* the life of Mother Earth? What is done to the poor is done to the earth, and what is done to the earth is done to the poor. Both are crucified. The poor are exploited when the earth is abused, for the poor and the earth are integrally connected. Mother Earth is strip-mined, her atmosphere contaminated, her waters polluted. Land is agro-business, crops are harvested for greatest profit, seas bilked for greatest yield. Can we take Mother Earth and her poor down from the cross? Is suffering redemptive? Is the cross life? We tread here in the realm of mystery; but a contemporary preaching of the cross that gives dignity to the poor, and the universe in all its glory, will integrally knit together the Incarnation and the Paschal Mystery. A life vivified by the Spirit, and the cross as consequence of that life well lived, will preach always on behalf of the life of the poor, out of life itself.

Latin American theology of the cross makes the cross of Jesus *real*. The real is Hope Embodied. The cross is not an antechamber to the resurrection but is united to it part and parcel, the outcome of preaching an enfleshed Jesus in the concrete, real life of the poor here and now—*la hora de los pobres*, the time of the poor, sings Gilmer Torres. The cross of Jesus is salvific in the Crucified *Pueblo*, who are themselves united to the Crucified Christ. They are *salus mundi*, as Ignacio Ellacuría writes, the salvation of the world.[4] The death of Jesus is real, the result of the proclamation of the reign of God; the Crucified *Pueblo* suffer the same lot:

> Jesus' death makes it clear why really proclaiming salvation runs up against the resistance of the world, and why the Reign of God does combat with the reign of sin. That is made manifest both in the death of the prophet, the one sent by God, and in the ravaging and death of humankind at the hands of those who make themselves gods, lording it over humankind. . . . [An] historic commitment to the crucified people makes it necessary to examine the theological meaning of this death . . . Reflecting historically on the death of Jesus helps us to reflect theologically on the death of the oppressed people, and the latter points back toward the former.[5]

The death of Jesus was the outcome of a life committed to the good news of justice. It does not "save" through the sacrificial shedding of blood but through the *life* of Jesus; the cross is consequence of that life. Life Incarnate saves and gives hope to the cosmos and to the poor. The Incarnate Jesus is the body of Christ crucified and identified with the Crucified *Pueblo*, saving consequence of life dedicated to the proclamation of the Reign.[6]

4. Ellacuria, "The Crucified People," 580–603.
5. Ibid., 586.
6. Ibid., 592–99.

Praedicatio Crucis

The Crucified people, the presence of the Suffering Servant, are the continuation of the salvific activity of Jesus:

> [T]he crucified people would be his (Jesus') continuation in history, and thus, we would not be talking about "another" servant. Hence, it would be sufficient to show that the crucified people combines some essential conditions of the Suffering Servant to show that the people constitute the most adequate site for the embodiment of the Servant, even if that is not true in all its fullness. ... [C]orrectly understood, this crucified people may be regarded as the most vital part of the church, precisely because it continues the passion and death of Jesus.[7]

We can no longer preach the atonement theologies of the past, turning Jesus into a holocaust offered to an angry God for the expiation of sin. If we are to rightly preach salvation and the cross today, we must go deeply into the meaning of atonement itself. Sacrifice is not given to placate an angry God; it is the consequence of *life* assumed by the God of love because of love. Salvation is not one moment in the life of an individual person saved from a wrathful God. It is the gift of the God of life and the Spirit of love living in the poor and all in solidarity with them. There is, then, no "preaching" of salvation by the preacher who ascends the pulpit on Sunday morning to belittle "unworthy" people because "Jesus died for you awful sinners." The preaching of the cross is the *praedicatio crucis*, the Holy Preaching, the poor preaching Church, the Crucified *Pueblo*. If our Sunday preaching is to survive in a meaningful way, it must be placed in solidarity with, and at the service of, the poor, the privileged presence of the crucified Risen One who, in the people, is the Holy Preaching.

---

7. Ibid., 601.

Chapter 4

Jesus Christ the *Nepantla* of God

Western thinking permeates contemporary global reality. Although the world is made up of many cultures, races, and languages, and there are many different approaches to reality, the Western scientific-technological-rational paradigm, with its intolerance of difference and variety, threatens to dominate the new global consciousness. This Western dominance is itself grounded in a world-view that is rooted in Greek philosophical thinking and a "Romanesque" swallowing up of difference into one large Empire. The New Empire consists of First World countries dominated by the United States and Europe. There are Asian players as well—countries like Japan, China, South Korea, and Taiwan. Laissez-faire capitalism, developed in the United States and Europe, has greatly affected the Asian economies. Many other countries vie to become part of this global empire—Brazil, Mexico, India, Indonesia, to name just a few. This new global capitalism, called "neo-liberal" by many, is a child of the Industrial Revolution and the old-style capitalism of the great tycoons of former centuries, monopolized by the United States and Europe. All schools of capitalism, in turn, are firmly rooted in the Roman Empire and ancient Greek categories of thinking.

A hallmark of the Western paradigm is dualism. Dualism is an attempt to explain the paradoxes of reality. How does one talk

Jesus Christ the *Nepantla* of God

about good and evil, sin and grace, spirit and matter, and at the same time make sense, find meaning, in a world otherwise viewed as confusing, changing, and meaningless? The classic metaphysical question of ancient Greek philosophy was: how to explain the "one" and the "many" without falling into chaos? There had to be a metaphysical "order." A thought system was necessary in order to make sense of reality.

However, the division of reality into dualisms would benefit neither philosophy nor theology—let alone the other sciences. In fact, it would be gravely harmful. New dualisms developed—like "science" and "metaphysics." Results were disastrous for religion and faith, and there were born yet other dualisms. One of the most destructive has been fundamentalism ("the Bible says that God created the world in seven days, so evolution is wrong") and relativism ("evolution has been scientifically proven, so the Bible is myth"). Relativism (Modernism, Liberalism) was associated with European theology, represented by Friedrich Daniel Ernst Schleiermacher (1768–1834), Adolf von Harnack (1851–1930), and Ignaz von Döllinger (1789–1890), among others.[1] Fundamentalism (Traditionalism, Conservatism) encompassed everyone from Karl Barth (far from fundamentalist!) to televangelists who mix politics and faith. There are bright lights on both sides. Karl Barth later looked favorably on Friedrich Schleiermacher and his lasting contribution to theology, while Ignaz Von Döllinger was truly a brilliant and creative theologian greatly misunderstood and feared by the conservative Catholic hierarchy of the time. Both sides include dangerous elements. Fundamentalism is disastrous to open and constructive dialogue, and relativism has little tolerance for stability. The irony is that fundamentalism can become a new relativism (only my view is absolute, everything else "relative"), and relativism a new fundamentalism ("my way or the high way"). Both end in dualism—the relativist pits science against faith by saying that all is "demythologized" by the scientific method, and the fundamentalist says that "atheistic science" is evil and "moralistic religion" good. The new dualisms, by and large, can be summarized

---

1. Consemius, "The Condemnation of Modernism," 14–26.

speaking of this one great post-modern dualism, science or faith: be either scientist or religious, you cannot be both, is the predominant assumption of this dualism.

Dualism is rooted in centuries of Western thought, although one could argue that true philosophy and theology have nothing to do with it. The prize for the most destructive dualism regarding the Christian faith, occurring again and again in Western history, goes to "matter" and "spirit." It permeates Western thinking. Some years ago, there was a fascination with angels in the United States. Perhaps this enthrallment with angelology was an attempt to escape the "material" realm of violence, war, disease, injustice, famine—all manifestations of evil and sin alive and well in our world. Angels are clean and pure, spiritual and perfect. Angels, in the various television series that presented them, were always young and beautiful, strong and handsome. There were no poor or diseased angels. This fascination with angels perhaps pointed to a popular belief that there was a singularly "spiritual" realm where creatures existed as "pure spirits."

The New Age obsession with angels paled into insignificance compared to other "matter-spirit" dualisms promulgated by the new religious fundamentalisms today. These, too, are rooted in Western civilization; the "good" (of course, those of *my* religion) are truly spiritual, while the "evil" (those outside of *my* religion) are worldly and bad. This New Fundamentalism, as present now to North American culture as were angels during their time, is more pernicious. It is closed, monolithic, conservative, and traditionalist, wanting to impose itself on everyone and everything in faith, society, and culture.[2]

Dualisms are regularly preached in North American churches. The New Age mentality, by and large not as prevalent today as some years back, has been replaced by rampant consumerism supported by the New Fundamentalism. It affects every aspect of

---

2. For an excellent analysis of the New Fundamentalism, see Marins, *Fundamentalismos*. There is also an fine video documentary done by James Carroll (*Constantine's Sword*) on anti-Semitism as manifested by a fundamentalist group who tried to "evangelize" the Air Force Academy in Colorado.

Jesus Christ the *Nepantla* of God

North American life from advertising to worship. The installation of air conditioning was regularly presented as an option for the few weeks of discomfort experienced in one of the parishes I pastored—in Seattle of all places! There was little questioning if it were an appropriate expenditure given the poverty of the urban area within the parish boundaries. For after all, if "material" bodies are comfortable during Sunday worship, we can be more "spiritual." Certainly we will not fall asleep during the preaching, which more often than not is, in fact, sleep inducing—a practical consequence of the matter-spirit dualism for the Holy Preaching! Advertising takes on strong aspects psychologically associated with worship and religion. Recently, I saw an advertisement for perfume in which a couple sprouted angelic wings and flew off together (to Paradise, I assume)! Go to many mega-churches in the United States, particularly those with fundamentalist leanings, and see the way the preacher is dressed, the exotic electronic equipment (once gigantic screen monitors were suggested for our sanctuary at a worship commission meeting because they had been seen at a neighboring mega-church). And if—God forbid—the preaching does not include the latest electronic gimmicks or any number of contemporary rhetorical devices, the congregation, it is commonly thought, will not pay attention. Preaching is emptied of faith and filled with fluff. No wonder we live in gnostic, dualistic illusions—precisely because that is where the preacher often lives. There are the other dualisms infecting the Sunday preaching in the First World—preacher and people, rhetoric and faith, Word and Sacrament, the presence of Christ in the Eucharist, or the community, or the preaching. The "where is Jesus?" dualism replaces the Real Presence of Christ in the community, animated by his Real Presence in the Word and the Sacrament of his Body and Blood.

A new theology of preaching is not only timely; it is necessary to our survival as a Church community in the twenty-first century. This new theology cannot tolerate any trace of the old dualistic theories of preaching. Nor can it be monistic. Rather, it must remind us constantly of the one and the many, not as either-or but both-and. This demands a revolutionary new move away from

Part One: In-Between

business as usual. We can no longer preach as we have—not even utilizing the best rhetorical techniques. We must move from Sunday preaching "as usual" to the *Holy Preaching*, the poor preaching Church, our call as followers of Jesus to solidarity with the poor.

Is it possible to overcome dualism in the Holy Preaching? Yes, I believe it is. But we must listen to the poor and cultures "foreign" to ours, we must open our hearts to radical *metanoia*—the change of heart that "stops us dead in our tracks and turns us one-hundred eighty degrees around in the other direction."[3] Perhaps this conversion from dualism to the poor community involves listening to the wisdom of indigenous Mexican culture (*nepantla*) and Asian wisdom ("creative polarity, *advaita*").

Two theologians among others have encouraged us to move away from destructive dualisms through reflection on the Incarnation and the Holy Trinity. *Nepantla* (Javier Garibay, SJ) and *advaita* (Raimon Panikkar) address dualism in all its forms, pointing toward an incarnational, Trinitarian approach to reality. Garibay has found *nepantla*—he defines the *Nahuátl* word as *unidad dual*, "dual unity"—especially helpful to Christology.[4] Jesus is the *Nepantla* of God. The two natures of the Second Person of the Holy Trinity, united in the dual unity of *nepantla*, provide an incarnational-methodological point of departure for all theology—indeed, all reality, says Garibay. His theology of *nepantla* can be useful for overcoming the dualism, for instance, between Word and Sacrament. The "dual unity" of the Person of Jesus can be described by referring to the role of Jesus as mediating Word and Sacrament who, with the Holy Spirit, is the "action" (José Comblin) of the Triune God whose universal will for the world is *life*, life in abundance (cf John 10:10)—in a word, *salvation*. Salvation is *concrete*. It cannot be divorced from life. Preaching is not just a series of words spoken by one person to a group of passive listeners. It is an active Word living in the people, concretely realized as

---

3. James G. Dunning, former director of the North American Forum for the Catechumenate, once described this as the definition of *metanoia*.

4. See Garibay, *Nepantla*, 322–25, 332–45, for a summary of Garibay's use of *nepantla* in Christology and Trinitarian theology.

Jesus Christ the *Nepantla* of God

the Sacrament that is Jesus and the Church, a mediating Word, a mediating Sacrament.

Jesus Christ is the *Nepantla* of God, dual unity of God and the human being—Mediator who "stands between" the creative poles of death and life, the human and the divine, the Word and the Sacrament, the Holy Preaching and the praxis that naturally flows from it. "*Jesus Christus ist der Mittler,*" says Dietrich Bonhoeffer—Jesus Christ is the Mediator.[5] This phrase forms a central part of his Christology. It is an important teaching of the New Testament. Jesus is the *Nepantla* of God, "one-hundred percent God, one-hundred percent us." God, in Jesus and by the breath of the Holy Spirit, becomes *who we are*—our hopes, our dreams, our culture, our history, our language, the color of our skin, all held together in a common, divine-humanity sanctified by the God who loves us beyond what we can imagine. "What was not assumed cannot be saved," St. Athanasius and the Fathers and Mothers of our earliest centuries rightly taught. God in Jesus "descends" in order to lift our humanity to divinity. How can it be that the Holy One would be "sullied" with "impure flesh"? But the Triune God from the beginning creates us in God's image (Gen 1:27). Flesh, from the very beginning, is holy because it is *imago Dei*. Jesus, the *Nepantla* of God, comes so that we can *remember* what we look like. We forget because of sin. Thus we do not recognize the presence of Jesus in the least (Matthew 25). We do not see the poor as human. We do not listen to the poor in the Holy Preaching. St. Paul teaches that *kenosis*, the "self-emptying" of God in Jesus, is God "vacating" divinity so that humanity is filled with God (Phil 2:5–11). How can God become human? How can a human being become God? In Jesus, the *Nepantla* of God, the dual unity of the divine-human is concretized in life. Jesus becomes poor, the Holy Preaching, the poor preaching Church.

A mediator is like a bridge. Javier Garibay calls Jesus the *Nepantla* of God, and Ramon Panikkar sees in Christology and Trinitarian theology—and all reality—the "creative polarities,"

---

5. This is a recurring theme in Bonhoeffer's theology. See, for example, his discussion of baptism in *DBW* 4: 221–22.

divine and human, which "hold" the Person of Jesus together and are so deeply rooted in the very being of the Holy Trinity and reality as a reflection of God:

> We are primarily concerned with the basic dignity of Man, because the person is a microcosm, a representation of the whole, a spark of never-ceasing fire. This cross-cultural image of Man could enable us to overcome the split of reality that so painfully tortures and threatens modernity. This image could transform the various dualities (*dvandva*)—resulting from a destructive break between Man and the earth, the subject and the object, understanding and love, arts and sciences, masculine and feminine—into creative polarities. This would also be true for the final break of reality, the one between Man and God, time and eternity, or Creator and creation. The *quaternitas perfecta* gives us a chance to discover an adequate human spirituality; it is the basis for a new spiritual attitude of the person to self, to the other, to the environment, and also to the all-embracing reality called God in many traditions.[6]

Panikkar uses the word *advaita* to express this "non-duality." It is especially significant when talking about the divine and the human in the Incarnate Jesus.[7]

St. Catherine of Siena's view of the Incarnation is likewise concrete and expresses reality as creative polarity. One of her favorite images is Jesus the Bridge.[8] Jesus is the one who "connects us" with God, with our truest self in God. A bridge connects two points that otherwise could not be accessed without great difficulty and many detours. A bridge transverses raging rivers; a bridge connects two islands; a bridge goes across a canyon, an abyss, connecting two separate but near areas so that they are accessible. As the God-human, Jesus, divine and human, bridges the chasm between God and humankind. As human he represents humanity to God, and as divine he represents God to humanity. He is the

---

6. Panikkar, *Opera Omnia*, 302–303.
7. Panikkar, *Christophany*, 23.
8. Catherine of Siena, *The Dialogue*, 64–160.

Jesus Christ the *Nepantla* of God

Bridge, says Catherine, the *Mittler*, the *Pons*, manifesting the dual unity, the *Nepantla*, the creative polarity of the divine-human at the deepest level:

> Catherine sees Jesus Christ as the connecting link, the Bridge, between limited human nature seeking self-understanding and unlimited divine nature offering that understanding. She insists there is no other way for human persons to relate to God in such a way that they can find and understand themselves, except through him. In Jesus she sees the embodiment of all that we seek. He is the one who, like us in all things except sin (Heb. 4:15), took human existence most seriously. He is the one who most fully sought and found self-understanding by relating intimately to the God whom he called "Father." Because of him and in him the human creature and God are no longer "poles apart."[9]

Later we will see how this creative polarity "self-communicates" as the Triune God in the *perichoeresis*—the interpenetrating relationships—of the three Persons, the model and point of contemplation for the Holy Preaching manifested in community.

If Christ is the Bridge, then perhaps the Church community are "bridge-builders," those who, with Jesus, work towards an integral dual unity and creative polarity in the world. A traditional title of the pope is *pontifex maximus*, the "great bridge-builder." We cannot possibly "construct" Jesus as a bridge is constructed, but if we are, as St. Paul says, the body of Christ (1 Cor 12:27), then we are *identified* with the presence of the Risen Christ in the world. We must "build" this presence, working to turn dualism into creative polarity—the synergy of the Mothers and Fathers. It is even appropriate, and perhaps necessary, to say that as the people of God, the body of Christ, and the Creation of the Holy Spirit, *we are the bridge*. Paul does not say we are "like" the body of Christ metaphorically. Paul says that we are *actually* the body of Christ. This is a point on which Dietrich Bonhoeffer insisted. Our work is one of bridge building, but we are also the bridge. We are the

---

9. O'Driscoll, "Catherine the Theologian," 4–17.

presence, verbal and sacramental, of the Bridge in the world. Ours is the work of reconciliation, love, justice, and peace. We are the Verbal Sacrament of Christ in the world—the sacramental presence of the Word in the Holy Preaching. Our call is to nepantlic dual-unity and creative polarity in the face of all dualism.

It is impossible to separate Jesus Christ and the Church community, Word and Sacrament, the divine and human natures of Jesus, the three Persons of the Holy Trinity, the world and all its people created by God in the communal image of the Triune God. All is held in *nepantla* and *advaita* by Jesus Christ, Son of the Living God and the Second Person of the Holy Trinity. The poor preaching Church is the *Sacra Praedicatio*, the Holy Preaching. The Church is "Christ existing as Church community," not an institution but a Living Person. We "are" this Person through the Holy Preaching, listening to the prophetic proclamation of the poor, in solidarity with the poor preaching Church, denouncing dualism and announcing that the world and all creation is infinite creative polarity united in the humanity of Jesus, the *Nepantla* of God.

Chapter 5

Sacramentum Mundi

The title of the encyclopedia of theology edited some years ago by the great Karl Rahner, SJ, expresses a reality that must never be forgotten in any epoch: *our world is sacramental* through and through. Jesus Christ, the living Bread, the Incarnate Word, is the "Sacrament of the encounter with God" (E. Schillebeeckx) in the world, for the world, to the world. The Church community is the Sacrament of Christ. From these two *"Ursakramente"* or *"Grundsakramente"*—the primary Sacraments—proceed a world shot through with sacramental intentionality. A sacrament is a concrete sign of God's love: "God so loved the world . . ." (John 3:16). The movement in liturgical and sacramental theology to a wider view of the sacraments has been nothing short of revolutionary, a veritable "post-modern sacramentology"[1] that sees the world-as-sacrament as *the* primary paradigm for contemporary sacramental theology.[2]

In the Catholic community, this new paradigm of sacrament began even before the Second Vatican Council, where the

---

1. Kadavil, *The World as Sacrament*, 16.
2. Ibid. Kadavil's entire book is based on the thesis that this "new" view is not new at all, but rooted in the early centuries of the Church and expressed primarily in the new liturgical theology (Alexander Schmemann) and the theology of liberation (Leonardo Boff).

sacramentality of Jesus and the Church were revisited by a theology previously hobbled by an overly dualistic view of the sacraments—a dualism that could not be resolved without serious theological reflection—centered primarily in a reductionist view of the "seven sacraments." The sacraments in the early Church were viewed in a holistic sense as the *mysterioi* (the Holy Mysteries), mysteries in which the presence of the Triune God were concrete but mysterious *signs* of God's love. St. Thomas Aquinas, though an important voice in Catholic sacramental theology, added categories of Aristotelian philosophy such as "substance" that, while important, muddied the waters of the sacramental mystery. It was the neo-Scholastics, though, who "demystified" the sacraments completely. *Ex opere operato* ("from the operation of the work," "by the very fact of the action being performed," what the sacrament effects through God's grace independent of the disposition of the minister or the recipient)[3] and *ex opere operantis* ("on account of the work of the one who works," stressing the importance of the disposition of the minister and the "recipient")[4] were split into irreconcilable dualism in which the *operato* took precedence over the *operantis*. The seven sacraments in the extreme then became "vehicles" that "imparted" the grace of God in a magical way that depended on the right action of the minister and, less, on the correct disposition of minister and recipient. The result was the definition from the old Baltimore Catechism I had to memorize as a child: "a sacrament is an outward sign instituted by Christ to give grace." Medieval scholastic theology coined special words to speak about sacramental reality, especially regarding the Eucharist. *Sacramentum* was the sacrament itself; *sacramentum et res* expressed the real presence of Christ; and *res sacramenti* was what the sacrament "effects" in the receiving individual and community.[5] This resulted in a strong but often lop-sided sense of physical devotion to the Eucharist elements of the consecrated bread and wine as the body and blood of Jesus; the *res sacramenti* was relegated to a distant second place.

3. *Catechism of the Catholic Church*, no. 1128.
4. McGrath, http://www.alistermcgrathwiley.com/glossary.asp
5. Seasoltz, *Living Bread*, 175–189.

Sacramentum Mundi

Theologians used philosophical and Greek metaphysical terms to express what happened when the priest prayed, on behalf of the people, the words of institution over the bread and wine. One of the most remembered (and debated!) words that attempted to describe the real presence of Christ in the Eucharist was "transubstantiation"—the substance of the bread and wine become the substance of the body and blood of Christ. Later centuries could not decipher the metaphysical category of substance in the same way and the word, when referring to the Eucharist, was used in an overly physical sense. The result was that the *mysterious sign* of the first centuries, so carefully crafted by our Fathers and Mothers, seemed forever lost.

But then came the Second Vatican Council and the sacramental theology that prepared its groundwork. Theologians like Otto Semmelroth, SJ, Karl Rahner, SJ, and Edward Schillebeeckx, OP, began to look at the earliest sources, especially the Scriptures and the Greek Fathers and Mothers, and reconnected Catholic theology with its roots. Jesus and the Church community were spoken of as *the* Sacraments *par excellence*. Sacramental theologians searched for new words that would express the real presence in the Eucharistic bread and wine in a way that kept with contemporary philosophy and experience, for instance, "transfinalization" or "transsignification" (a word popularized by Schillebeeckx[6]), stressing the *sacramental* presence of Christ in the Eucharist. This openness to a wider view of sacramentality has reaped a great harvest. Jesus and the Church community were seen as the Sacraments from which all others proceeded; but recently, aside from this eventful return to the sources, the mystery of the sacraments has developed such that the reign of God is itself a sacrament in Latin American theology (Victor Codina, SJ), and, even more significantly, the world, all creation, and the cosmos itself:

> This broader view of the sacramentality of Christ and
> the Church equally undergirds the importance of
> the signification of sacrament in the world. It shows that
> the human relationship to God and to the world is an

---

6. Ibid.

important concern in the understanding of the sacraments. Negatively, these paradigms set certain limitations, and are confined to the boundaries of the adherents of the Christian faith. For this reason, we should look for a new paradigm which will be able to address the issue of the significance of sacraments in the world and the possibility of going beyond the confines of the Church.[7]

Catholics are especially fond of using this enhanced concrete sacramental language. The two primary sacraments, Christ and the Church community, are prior to the others—the seven sacraments (Baptism, Confirmation, Holy Eucharist, Reconciliation, Anointing of the Sick, Holy Orders, and Matrimony), but also the reign of God, the world, all creation. Nor can sacramentals (the new word "parasacraments" seems contrived) be forgotten—holy water, images of saints, prayers, etc. This enhanced Catholic sacramental theology posits that all reality is sacramental, for all things have the concrete capacity to reveal the love, justice, and mercy of the Triune God.

Catholics are not the only Christians who have this strong bent toward the sacraments. The Orthodox community and the Eastern Churches have celebrated the "Sacred Mysteries" for as long as the West and enjoy the same sacramental system. The Protestant community is strongly sacramental as well, particularly the historic Reformation Churches (Martin Luther's commentaries on the sacraments show how strong!).

The bishops at the Second Vatican Council, in their first major document (*Sacrosanctum Concilium*), spoke of several "real presences" of Christ in the Eucharist: the presence of Christ in the Word, in the consecrated bread and wine, in the ministers, and in the celebrating people. These "real presences" are *all* sacramental, concrete signs of God's love manifesting the presence of Christ and the Holy Spirit among the people. While the real presence of Christ in the Eucharistic bread and wine enjoy "privilege of place," the others, in the Word and the community, are also real presences of the sacramental Christ.

7. Ibid., 81.

Sacramentum Mundi

In fidelity to the Catholic sacramental tradition, I have elsewhere referred to the real presence of Christ in the Word, using a word similar to St. Augustine's "inverbation." "Transverbation" attempts to describe, in sacramental categories, the real presence of Christ in the Word—an ontological, substantial, sacramental change in the Word of the Scriptures and the preaching such that it becomes the real presence of Jesus.[8] The real presence of Christ in the worshipping community can likewise be described as "transecclesiation," that is, an ontological, substantial, sacramental change in the community such that the people become the sacramental presence of Christ in the world. This has especially profound meaning for the poor preaching Church. Perhaps two more words can be coined for the sacramental view described above: "transpauperation," the real sacramental presence of Christ in the poor; and "transuniversation," the real presence of Christ in the entire universe.

The Scriptural basis for the real presence of Christ in the Church community (transecclesiation) is St. Paul's "the body of Christ." In First Corinthians (12:27) Paul says, "*You are* the body of Christ." There is debate over exactly what Paul means. Is he using metaphor? Simile? "You are *like*, you are *similar to*, the body of Christ"? Some hold this opinion. However, I believe that Paul says exactly what he means: "You *are* the body of Christ." Two theologians among others (Dietrich Bonhoeffer[9] and Jerome Murphy O'Conner[10]) have maintained that Paul is not using metaphor—the Church community *is* the actual, real presence of Christ. Bonhoeffer's theological preoccupation with the Church community as the body of Christ points to his ever-increasing concern for that which was *real*. The Church is "Christ existing as Church community." Likewise, we can rightly say that Christ's real presence is the concrete poor person (transpauperation), with whom Jesus literally identifies (Matt 25:40). This Scriptural reference to the presence of Christ in the poor is supported by many others. Like the body

---

8. Pastro, *Enflamed*, 72–75.
9. *DBWE* 14:446–455.
10. Seasoltz, *Living Bread, Saving Cup*, 1–30.

of Christ as the Church community, it is not simply metaphorical. The poor person *is* the real presence of Christ. Jon Sobrino says that the crucified body of Jesus means little unless it has "historical reality" in the poor.[11] The sacramental presence of Christ permeates the entire universe—the endangered cosmic community, the endangered poor, endangered Mother Earth. A rediscovery of the sacramental in the community, in the poor, and in the universe is a major task of the new theological paradigm. Can we see sacramental reality as it *is*, not locking it into traditional language and categories that stupefy without liberating? Schillebeeckx wrote the following prophetic words in his doctoral dissertation:

> On the basis of the sacramental structure of revelation, i.e., by the fact that the divine manifests itself in the forms and shapes of *our* earthly reality it is immediately evident that the material object of revelation always is the divine reality, as a reality immediately relevant to us: God as *our* God, the "Deus salutaris," so that this aspect of salvation is *essential* for the constitution itself of the material object of faith. We believe in *earthly* realities as visible, tangible, audible mysteries or manifestations of supernatural realities of faith.[12]

Sacraments are expressions of reality; but more than expressions, they are *reality itself*. The Holy Preaching as the sacramental presence of Christ, the Church, the reign of God, and the universe are not individual separate voices but a veritable sacramental chorus of praise. Jesus Christ is the Sacrament of God; the Church is the Sacrament of Jesus; we, sisters and brothers of Christ, are sacraments of the Crucified and Risen One who live in a world, a cosmos, a reality, that is itself *sacramental*. All is *sacramentum mundi*, sacrament of the world, sacrament of the poor, sacrament of the *pueblo*, sacrament of the cosmos—the Holy Preaching for the world and the poor.

---

11. Sobrino, *Jesus the Liberator*, 254.
12. Schillebeeckx, *The Schillebeeckx Reader*, 77.

Chapter 6

Preaching as Dialogue

The word "homily" means conversation—a simple dialogue. A dialogue involving listening and speaking is non-dualistic but never one-sided. It is dual unity, *nepantla*, a communion of two different points of view brought together by holistic speech. The homily, too, is dialogic. It can never be simple monologue where the "preacher" gives religious truths to passive listeners. Our tradition has not often seen the Holy Preaching holistically. Seldom is the Sunday preaching a dialogue.

What would happen if we returned to the roots of the ancient word in order to discover anew the Holy Preaching? For even when the Holy Preaching is the traditional Sunday sermon, there can be profound dialogue at work. It will help the preacher—and the preaching community—to reflect on how this conversation, this dialogue, unfolds.

In April 1707, George Friedrich Handel (1685–1759) composed *Dixit Dominus*, a choral setting of Psalm 109.[1] The phrase *Dixit Dominus* ("The Lord says") dominates the first part. *Dixit* is repeated over and over. *Dixit Dominus*—God says, God speaks. Our ancient belief is that God is not silent. God speaks. We, God's

---

1. http://imslp.org/wiki/Dixit_Dominus,_HWV_232_(Handel,_George_Frideric).

Part One: In-Between

holy people the preaching Church, listen—and respond. Our dialogue is with the Triune God, the poor, creation.

Theology is never consigned only—or primarily—to the academy. In the early centuries, the Fathers and Mothers spoke of theology as "the contemplation of the Holy Trinity." Theology is lived in the life of the people, in the life of the Church community. It has been pointed out that the Fathers and Mothers generally did not teach in the academy. Rather, they *preached* in the midst of the people of God. St. John Chrysostom (347–407), perhaps the greatest preacher in Christian history, *did* theology by a Holy Preaching in dialogue with the people. The homiletic dialogue with the people was the icon (Bruno Forte), the image, of the *perichoeresis* within the Holy Trinity. The Fathers and Mothers rightly understood that theology could not be divorced from the people or its intimate connection with the Triune God. Archbishop Joseph Raya, when referring to St. John the Evangelist, calls every theologian a "troubadour of love, a singer of love."[2]

Is the Holy Preaching a "contemplation of the Trinity"? This question must be relentlessly pursued if we are to understand the dynamics of preaching and approach it as the life-blood of the Triune God in the people. A living theology of proclamation must be recovered if the Holy Preaching is to survive into the twenty-first century and beyond—a theology significantly different, rooted in the Trinitarian contemplation of the Fathers and Mothers.

If preaching is dialogue, if theology is contemplation of the Holy Trinity, some time must be spent developing a Trinitarian approach to the Holy Preaching. This approach will be rooted in ecclesiology, which, strictly speaking, *is* theology proper and its only *raison d' être*.

Western thought views dialogue largely from an analytical perspective, the viewpoint of the subject, asking questions like: "*what* is the function of dialogue, *how* does dialogue happen, *in what* does dialogue consist, *why* does dialogue happen"? They approach dialogue from the philosophical viewpoint rooted in the Greco-Roman tradition of "question-answer" and the priority

2. Raya, *The Transfiguration*, 51.

Preaching as Dialogue

of the subject. In this analytic approach, the question is mostly static; and the answer even more so. Dialogue becomes *monologue*. Monologue never listens. In monologue, the subject is all-important; the other loses ground quickly. Think of how often you are a "step ahead" in conversation, even with your closest friends. We even complete the sentences of our "dialogue" partners before they are finished! The Holy Preaching, a dialogue meant to have a conversational tone understood by all—children, poor, women, men—often ends in monologue, the ordained preacher the only "partner" who understands what is said! The exceptions—like John Chrysostom, Antonio de Montesinos, and Dietrich Bonhoeffer—are few. In this dialogue, the *real* conversation is that of the Triune God—which the preacher and the preaching people "overhear." Antonio de Montesinos understood this ("I am the voice of Christ crying in the wilderness") when he stepped into the pulpit during Advent of 1511 to denounce the oppression wrought by the Spaniards upon the *Taíno* indigenous of the island of *Quisquella*, and Dietrich Bonhoeffer when he preached resistance to the Nazi oppression.

The preaching giants of our tradition were great because they knew the importance of *listening*. Human dialogue at its best can reflect the *perichoeresis* of the Holy Trinity, participating by grace, as St. Maximus Confessor says, in the *one* Word spoken by the Trinity. St. Ephrem the Syrian uses a vivid image: When teaching us to speak, God holds a mirror in front of God's divinity, and the reflecting surface points toward us, as when one teaches a parrot to speak. We are slow learners, but God is patient and loving. God *listens*. God has spoken one Word; it reverberates in the *perichoeresis* of the Holy Trinity.

How do we listen to one another? How do we converse with one another? Dietrich Bonhoeffer writes from prison that the Christianity of the future will be less formal preaching and more "prayer and doing God's justice."[3] Prayer—the "contemplation of the Holy Trinity"—can only happen through silent waiting, as

---

3. *DBWE* 8:390.

Part One: In-Between

Bonhoeffer says.[4] Action for justice requires prayer and contemplation in silence before the living God. We also need to practice silent listening before one another. Our culture reacts against silence. It needs to be nurtured intentionally—particularly in our places of worship.

Recently, I was present at the blessing of a public locale sponsored by a Church group. As the deacon was proclaiming the gospel (incidentally, Matt 25:31–46), the cell phone of one of the staff rang. She rose, went off to the side where everyone could still see and hear her, and . . . answered the telephone! Silence eludes us, even in our worship. The Triune God, though, *listens in the silence of the Word*. God *hears* the cry of the poor (Pss 34:17, 69:33). God *hears* the widow, the orphan, and the immigrant (Exod 22:22–23, Deut 10:18, Zech 7:10, Jer 7:6). God *hears* the request of Abraham and Sarah for a child (Gen 17:16). God *hears* the Israelites enslaved in Egypt (Exod 3:7). The Scriptures are filled with the speaking God who *listens in silence*. We, icons of the God who listens, need to practice once again the art of listening if we are to become the preaching Church.

What if the preaching Church nurtured "ears to hear" (Matt 11:15, 13:9, Mark 4:9, Rev 3:22) and a heart for dialogue? What if people were taken seriously as active participants in the Holy Preaching? What if we "overheard" the *perichoeresis* of the Divine Three in the poor, in creation, in one another? Perhaps these questions can form a "starting point" for a reevaluation of the theology of preaching that "speaks" to people of the twenty-first century—particularly the poor, the immigrant, indigenous peoples, women, people alienated because of sexual preference, and many others. Can we see that the Holy Preaching is icon of the Dialogue in the innermost depths of the Holy Trinity? Can we catch the "energies" (St. Gregory Palamas) of the grace of the conversation?

Perhaps it is blasphemous to think that can unravel the conversation of the community of the three Living Persons. We can be sure, however, of the Word "uttered" in that sacred space: Jesus. Theologians from Aquinas to Rahner have maintained that this is

---

4. De Lange, *Waiting for the Word*.

Preaching as Dialogue

the Word spoken by God, resounding in mystery, never exhausted by other words. That is why God is reticent to speak and quick to listen in silence. Karl Rahner speaks of the silence of God in eternity, "where the only Word spoken is Jesus Christ, reverberating through the ages."[5] All other words pass through this Word, spoken at the dawn of creation,[6] to the Patriarchs and Matriarchs, Moses and Miriam, the Prophets, the tender love and mercy of God's Word spoken at Bethlehem, in the life, death, and resurrection of Jesus, in the Incarnate One present with us.

We often think of dialogue as a "resolution" between two people, an "agreement" reached by parties in which there is a *via media* often agreeable to neither but adopted so that things can move forward. However, there is only one *via* in real dialogue— the *via trinitaria*. In the ancient tradition, God, the Living Three, is eternal dialogue of silent *perichoeresis* filled with sonorous music (St. John of the Cross). It is important for us to attend in prayer and contemplation to the conversation if there is any hope of our true listening to the Holy Preaching.

The preaching Church in dialogue is a people whose action is integral part of the preaching event. The dialogue is Trinitarian by its very nature: the Triune God, the poor community, and the world God has created. The Living Three speaks the Word to the Church community; the Church community listens and participates by grace; and the community of the Holy Preaching acts on behalf of the poor and the world community. The dialogue implies a special openness on the part of the Church community—to the God who speaks the Word and listens in silence, to the Incarnate Word divinely spoken, to the poor seeking the justice of God's reign, and to the world created by the God of love. Church community and ordained preacher are one community of the baptized in dialogue, one preaching Church; the goal of the Sunday preaching is animation of the preaching Church of the poor toward loving action in

---

5. I read this quote many years ago but have been unable to locate it. I believe it is from *Encounters with Silence*.

6. See *DBWE* 3:40-44 for Bonhoeffer's exposition of the creating Word.

the world. The *Sacra Praedicatio* in dialogue, part and parcel of the world beloved of God, listens and acts.

Part Two

WITHIN

The Holy Preaching is *holy* because it is the community gathered in prayer and proclamation, a people that "does" the theology of the Mothers and Fathers—contemplation of the Holy Trinity. Contemplation—as José Comblin envisions it—is prayerful, an action that looks not at an object (as if the Holy One could be objectified) but an "inner experience" of the Spirit.[1] The Holy Preaching, the preaching Church of the poor, is the community at prayer. St. Paul encourages us to "pray always" (1 Thess 5:17), reminding us that prayer is not so much "time spent" but activity involving reflected *discipleship*.

Preaching is paramount among these activities. The Holy Preaching is "holy praying" in community, among a people. No one person is privileged. The center of the *within* of the Holy Preaching is neither preacher, nor listener, nor text; rather, the center is the Holy Preaching itself, the community who is the body of Christ. The Spirit prays within the people in "sighs too deep for words," moving the community to look to the "within"—"Likewise the Spirit helps us in our weakness; for we do not know how to pray as we ought, but that very Spirit intercedes with sighs too deep for words. And God, who searches the heart, knows what is the mind of the Spirit, because the Spirit intercedes for the saints

1. See Comblin, *La Vida*.

according to the will of God" (Rom 8:26–27). The Spirit moves the community to *preach* through life and prayer, not with words but through "the cries of the poor" (cf Ps 34) in action for justice.

A number of years ago, I had a conversation with Gonzalo Ituarte, OP, at the time Dominican Provincial of Mexico. For many years, he served as pastor in Chiapas, where he was also the Vicar General for Don Samuel Ruiz, the "bishop of the poor" in the Diocese of San Cristobal. Fr. Ituarte described how the Holy Preaching happened in the rural parish communities of Chiapas. After the Liturgy of the Word, everyone, including the presbyter presiding at the Eucharist, sat in a circle. Beginning with the elders, they shared events from their lives from the previous week in the light of the Scripture. What did God's holy Word have to say about my infant daughter's intestinal infection? About a *patrón* who had taken advantage of me in the workplace? Why was I unable to sell my corn and coffee for a fair price? Why was the military presence greater in the village last week? These and many other issues were brought to the Sunday preaching, much like the communities that Ernesto Cardenal described in Nicaragua some years ago.[2] *Campesino* communities *became* the Holy Preaching. Although the presbyter coordinated, there was no one "preacher." The Holy Preaching was the Word proclaimed by the poor preaching Church, reflecting on the praxis of the past week and proposing renewed action for justice. Fr. José Marins describes a similar methodology with the Base Ecclesial Communities he mentors.

In this methodology, the preaching Church of the poor is invited to prayerful reflection within the lived community. This look "within" happens in the context of the Sunday liturgy (in rural areas these liturgies are often coordinated by a catechist), a celebration of prayer including the proclamation of the Word and the sharing of the Eucharist that enables the community to prepare for the coming days—to be the Holy Preaching through the lived praxis of the community at prayer. The Holy Spirit inspires the look within, in both prayer and praxis of the preaching Church of the poor. The Spirit moves the community to look inward but

---

2. See *The Gospel of Solentiname*.

Part Two: Within

also inspires the preaching Church to act for justice. José Comblin, Victor Codina, SJ, Leonardo Boff, and other Latin American theologians say that now more than ever, the need in theology is for a renewed "pneumatology" (Panikkar uses the word "pneumalogy"[3]) where the Spirit, acting in the people, takes center stage "in Christ." The Holy Preaching can never be divorced from the Holy Spirit. Looking deep within, we see traces of the Spirit who inspires the "look outward" for justice. We go with Jesus into the desert, driven by the Spirit (Mark 1:12) to the *within*.

---

3 Panikkar, *Christophany*, 10.

Chapter 7

Locus Theologicus
Paying Attention

Gregory Heille, OP, says that the first thing taught in a homiletic classroom is "paying attention."[1] Homiletic "paying attention" is an attitude toward life in which small details otherwise overlooked bubble up into the preacher's field of vision. Contemplation is this "paying attention." The contemplative life for the Holy Preaching, the preaching Church of the poor, is learning to pay attention to the seemingly "insignificant," the *Deus Absconditus*, as Martin Luther insisted—the "hidden God." What does the journey into the deepest self mean for the individual preacher? Is there a "deepest self" in the preaching Church as a *pueblo*? What does this "within" look like? How do we develop an attitude toward life that gives priority to this contemplative "paying attention"?

A *locus theologicus* is the "place" from which theology is done. Our tradition has cited many.[2] What are the *loci theologici*, of the Holy Preaching? Where do we "pay attention"? Since the theology of the Fathers and Mothers is "the contemplation of the

1. Heille, *Theology of Preaching*, 11.

2. See, for instance, a fine essay by Torres, "La Familia as Locus Theologicus," 444–61.

Locus Theologicus

Holy Trinity," this "look within" discerns the presence of Christ and the action of the Holy Spirit in the world and among the poor and adopts a stance of prayerful contemplation in order to name the *loci theologici* for the Holy Preaching.

In many traditional homiletic classrooms in the United States and the First World, the *loci theologici* are three: the text, the preacher, and the listener. While not denying that these can and must be places from where a theology of preaching is done, I will, at the same time, suggest some alternatives.

First, is there an overall *locus* for the theology of preaching? I believe there is. At the risk of tautology, the *locus theologicus* for the theology of preaching is: the *Holy Preaching itself*. This *locus* suggests many other *loci*. I will concentrate on several. Two overlap with the classic *loci theologici* of the theology of liberation: the Church and the poor.[3] The others are: word, people, and cosmos. While these *loci* by no means exhaust the many places from which the theology of preaching can be done, they provide a possible starting point for the look "within" the Holy Preaching. They form inclusive avenues of reflection that open many possibilities.

The Holy Preaching is *the locus* for the theology of preaching. Some years ago, Paul Janowiak, SJ, wrote an excellent study on the theology of preaching. The overall *locus* for Janowiak's profound theology is the Holy Preaching—the title of this monumental work.[4] The book revolves around the integrity of the Holy Preaching. The Holy Preaching cannot be parsed out into an individual homily or "preaching event." It does not revolve around the text, the preacher, or the listener alone. It is not one moment on a Sunday morning disconnected from the life of preacher and listener (both of whom form only parts of the Holy Preaching). Neither can it be simply a "bridge" between the Liturgy of the Word and the Liturgy of the Eucharist. It is, rather, an integral whole that is part and parcel with the Eucharist, Christ's Real Presence permeating Eucharist, community, and universe, also present in a unique and mysterious way in the Holy Preaching, whose original

---

3. Gutiérrez, *The Theology of Liberation*, 15.
4. Janowiak, *The Holy Preaching*.

Part Two: Within

meaning postulated by St. Dominic of Guzman, the founder of the Dominicans, was the *community itself*. The Sunday preaching is inseparable from the entire liturgical celebration and Christ's Real Presence, itself inseparable from the poor, the community, indeed, the entire universe. In an essay written a few years later, Janowiak says:

> Liturgical memory and practice cradle our immediate reality and invite its transformation and consecration, and—out of the context of our faithful gathering—originate the future hopes and dreams of a waiting world. Any sacramental claims we make today about the real presence of Christ in the liturgy must embrace this relational, dialogical and participative shape, which springs from God's unquenchable desire to be in relationship with us, in and with Christ, through the indwelling grace of the Holy Spirit.[5]

The Holy Preaching was the original name for the Order of Preachers—women preceding men by ten years![6] The theology of preaching is not determined solely by the text, the listener, the preacher, or the preaching event. Preacher, listener, text, and event all form part of the wider Church community, the human community, the universe. The moments devoted to the Sunday preaching are inseparable from the entire Eucharistic liturgy. According to ancient tradition, there is really only *one Eucharist*, celebrated by the risen Jesus in the presence of the Holy Trinity and the *sanctorum communio*. Our Eucharistic celebration on Sundays—word, preaching, sacrament, community, and ritual—is but a reflection of that one Eucharist celebrated by Jesus in the presence of the community of the Holy Trinity and the community of the saints. The one Eucharist includes us, the celebrating community of saints in our parish churches and places of worship.[7] That celebration is, in turn, the celebration of the entire universe permeated with the

---

5. Paul A. Janowiak, "Running to Communion," 16.

6. Prouille, still an active community of Dominican women, was Dominic's first foundation.

7. Corbon, *The Wellspring of Worship*.

Locus Theologicus

Real Presence of Christ. The Holy Preaching, an expression of the Eucharistic Real Presence, feeds the Church community through Word and Sacrament. It is THE *locus theologicus* of the theology of preaching. In it, we "pay attention" to all the *loci theologici* that surround us—and what the *loci* reflect: the Holy Trinity.

The Living Three, according to José Comblin, is never an object. But if theology is the "contemplation of the Holy Trinity," the Triune God is *the* center from which we speak of all *loci theologici*. Bruno Forte says that the Church community is the "icon" of the Holy Trinity; so the Triune God, contemplated in the Church community, is the measure of *any* theology of preaching, *any* Christology, *any* ecclesiology. The Holy Trinity has been the subject of Christian theology from the time of the Cappadocians to the contemporary theological reflections of Raimon Panikkar and Catherine Mowry LaCugna. The Holy Trinity is Oneness and Community together, Three Living Persons, unique, distinct, and different, yet one God, one perfect community, a God of relationship whose community "spills over" into all humanity, all creation—and to those who dare its contemplation: "Christ reclines his head on a patient spirit (cf. Matt. 8:20), and an intellect at peace becomes a shelter of the Holy Trinity."[8] All things proceed from the Trinity and return to the Trinity, the classic *exitus et reditus*, all things, all creation, all humanity, the entire universe.

I have already referred to Jesus as the *Nepantla* of God. He is the Sacramental *Word* of the God of the poor. The Incarnate Word reminds us that the word—Scriptural, preached, written, spoken, heard—is *locus* for the theology of preaching. To look more closely at this *locus*, we look to the Person of Jesus.

Perhaps it is best not to rehash traditional Christology—the "study" of Christ—as if the Second Person of the Trinity could be studied! Raimon Panikkar has, rather, suggested that "Christophany" may be a more appropriate word to speak about what it is we do when the Person of Jesus is reflected on through theological eyes.[9] Christophany, says Panikkar, delves into the realm

---

8. Evagrius of Pontus: *The Greek Ascetic Corpus*, 80.
9. Panikkar, *Christophany*, 3–35.

Part Two: Within

of the human experience of Christ's epiphany. The question is not the "how" of the Incarnation or the "who" of the historical Jesus. Rather, where is the risen Jesus manifested in our life, our community, the poor, and the world, *today*? The epiphany of Jesus Christ in our world today is a Christophanic concern and was *the* primary question for Dietrich Bonhoeffer, who began his lectures on Christology by asking, "Who is Jesus Christ for us *today*?"[10] Bonhoeffer felt that we best know Jesus by looking for his presence in the *context* we *live*. For him, that meant the Nazi regime in Germany and the concomitant disregard for the "victim"— the Jewish people. Where is Christ's presence discerned? For Raimon Panikkar, traditional Christology concentrates on the "what" and the "how" to the detriment of the *real* "Who." The Who is not discerned simply by looking at the "historical Jesus" as we *think* he existed two thousand years ago in Palestine. The sources for this "Who" are small indeed, confined to the words of Jesus in the gospel, some early reflections of the Christian community, and scant historical references such as Josephus. Panikkar, rather, prefers to speak of the "Christic experience," or "event," that "explodes" the historic time of the Incarnation (history, he says, is a Western invention and cannot be sole representative of Reality). The Christic event is pan-historical, pan-cultural, and pan-temporal. It occurs anywhere and everywhere and is not confined to the "Christian community." The work of the Holy Spirit is to point us in the right direction: where do we look for the Christic event?[11]

Bonhoeffer says that preaching is "the living Christ walking among the people." Preaching is the living presence of Christ— and the Holy Spirit who inspires, in freedom (cf. Gal 5:1), word, hearing, and action. The liturgical presence of Christ, as Vatican II says, is not confined to the elements of the consecrated bread and wine. It is found in the word and the preaching ("transverbation"), in the ministers who celebrate liturgy *in persona Christi*, in the worshipping community ("transecclesiation"), which Panikkar

---

10. See *DBW* 12:280–289.
11. Panikkar, *Christophany*, 143–184.

Locus Theologicus

calls now not *alter Christus* but *ipse Christus*),[12] as well as in the consecrated bread and wine. The Real Presence of Christ is manifested in the entire liturgy, including the preaching, in the Holy Preaching that is the community. The Holy Spirit gives birth to the community.[13] If, as Panikkar's Christophany posits, the Christic event is the presence of Jesus everywhere, not confined to any one history or culture, is not Christ present in the Holy Preaching, the poor preaching Church? There is an *incarnatio continuo*, as Panikkar says. Or perhaps with Martin Luther, we can speak of the *Deus Absconditus*, the God who comes and "hides" in Jesus. In Pauline *kenosis* (Phil 2:5–11), Jesus "empties" himself of divinity, becoming nothing so that we can become everything. God in Jesus, by the working of the Holy Spirit, comes and "hides" in the Holy Preaching. Vatican II reminds us of the Real Presence of Christ in word, sacrament, and community. The liturgy is an expression of our life. If the Sunday liturgy is a reflection of the one divine Eucharist celebrated by Jesus in the presence of the Holy Trinity and the *communio sanctorum*, how much more is Reality a reflection of the divine liturgy celebrated by Christ, the *ipse Christus*, the Real Presence of Christ in the universe, filling all things (cf Eph 1:23)—including (and perhaps even especially) the words through which we speak of the Christic event.

Another *locus* of the Holy Preaching is the Church community, the people of God, much more than simple "listener" to the Sunday preaching. The *pueblo* is active participant, impelled to action by the Spirit. The Holy Preaching is the preaching Church of the poor, the community that follows Jesus the Master. This community is not static. The Church, Bonhoeffer says, is not an institution but a Person. A person lives and breathes and moves. A person is alive. The Church is a Person, the Holy Preaching of Christ, *Wort* of God, *Antwort* of the people, the Christ spoken by God who returns to God in the answer that is the collective response of the people (Semmelroth, Janowiak). Liturgy is life enlivened by the Spirit and enfleshed by Jesus in the people of God. How can we

---

12. Panikkar, *A Dwelling Place for Wisdom*, 102.
13. Comblin, *The Holy Spirit and Liberation*.

Part Two: Within

be attentive to the presence of Christ in the community, the Holy Preaching, the Christic event enlivening every heart?

Can we speak of "ecclesiophany"? Ecclesiology is traditionally a "reasoned word" about the Church. But where is the Church community *manifested* in the world? Where is it *experienced*? When Panikkar speaks about the Church, he refers to St. Bonaventure's *ecclesia ab Abel*—the "Church from Abel."[14] The Church community cannot be restricted to a specific culture at a specific time of history. The doctrine of *sanctorum communio* already points to this wider view of the Church. When we ask, "what is the Church," or "how is the Church constituted," we are dealing with ecclesiology. Ecclesiophany asks, *Where* is the Church community *manifested* and *experienced*?" Where is the Church community *present*? Where do we see, taste, smell, hear, the Church community? How is the Church community active in the world? How is the Church community part of the world community? These are different questions, more profound, less specific. At the same time, they do not turn the Church into the reign of God. Ecclesiophany will not identify the Church community with the kingdom. Rather, the people of God are a "leaven" for the God's reign; the Church community is "salt of the earth" and "light of the world" (Matt 5:14). Where is the Church community *manifested*? Is it theologically more accurate to speak of an *ecclesia ab Abel*, a people that is present and made manifest at all times and places, regardless of culture, time, and history? Ecclesiophany will not limit the Church to its Western manifestations. Instead, it will allow for the manifestation of the community in those places where the West sometimes fails to look—culture and the poor. Ecclesiophany invites us to open the Holy Preaching to the *locus* of the entire cosmos. As we cannot limit Jesus and the Holy Spirit, we cannot limit the Church community—nor the cosmos. The cosmos, the universe itself, is *locus* for the work of the poor preaching Church.

No one *locus* is more important than the other. But we are called to make the *option for the poor*, and that will mean paying special attention to the poor. This option is made first by the Triune

---

14. Panikkar, *Il Cristo Sconosciuto*, 97.

Locus Theologicus

God. Since the Church community is the icon of the Holy Trinity, the divine option for the poor must also be *our* option. Certainly Latin American theologies such as the theology of liberation, indigenous theology, and eco-feminism, as well as *any* theology done in the context of poverty, have reflected on the poor as *locus theologicus*. The poor must always be a primary *locus* for theology, and, likewise, they must be a central *locus* for the theology of the Holy Preaching. The preaching Church recognizes and celebrates the poor as special evangelizers of the Church community. The Fathers and Mothers made an option for the poor. Sts. Basil the Great, John Chrysostom, Gregory of Nyssa, Ephrem the Syrian, Origen, and many more, dedicated much of the Holy Preaching to the poor. It will be fitting to conclude this chapter by "paying attention" to the words of St. John Chrysostom regarding Lazarus and the Rich Man (Luke 16:19–31):

> For all this let us give thanks to God who loves (hu)mankind. Let us gather help from the narration. Let us talk of Lazarus continually in councils, at home, in the marketplace, and everywhere. Let us examine carefully all the wealth which comes from this parable, so that we may both pass through the present troubles without grief and attain to the good things which are to come: of which may we all be found worthy, by the grace and love of our Lord Jesus Christ, with whom to the Father, together with the Holy Spirit, be glory, honor, and worship, now and ever, and unto ages of ages. Amen.[15]

Can we, who have such a rich tradition of the option for the poor, afford to ignore Lazarus and the poor any longer in our preaching? More importantly, can we afford not to listen as *they* preach the Gospel to the dominant culture, inviting us to look anew at ancient *loci theologici*?

---

15. St. John Chrysostom, *On Wealth and Poverty*, 38.

Chapter 8

The Holy Preaching
Who not How

On March 13, 2013, Jorge Mario Bergolio, the Archbishop of Buenos Aires in Argentina, stepped out onto the papal balcony in simple white robes after being elected the two-hundred forty-sixth pope of the Roman Catholic Church. The reporters and the world gasped, because few knew this man—he was not often mentioned as *papabile*, although it was rumored that he was a runner up in the conclave that elected Josef Razinger, Pope Benedict XVI, some years before. Francis, the name he selected, was inspired by his friend Cardinal Claudio Hummes, who told him: "Do not forget the poor." Pope Francis looked serenely over the vast throng in the *piazza* of St. Peter's. After saying a few simple words, he did something no other pope in the history of the Catholic Church has done—he bowed and asked for the blessing and prayers of the people.

We soon learned who this man was—a Jesuit, a teacher, a theologian, a religious superior, an Argentinian immigrant born of Italian parents, a pastor, a man who had worked with the poor. Although he is eminently pastoral and down to earth, he is also among the most theologically savvy popes ever. His favorite image of Church is the people of God, richly scriptural and taken

The Holy Preaching

from the Second Vatican Council's Dogmatic Constitution on the Church, *Lumen Gentium*. The poor are intimately related to his vision of the Church community. In his first few days as pope, he said, "How I desire a poor Church of the poor."

But his most revealing statements about the Church community are found in the apostolic exhortation, *Evangelii Gaudium*, "The Joy of the Gospel," promulgated on the feast of Christ the King in November of 2013. He calls the Church an "evangelizing community," a community called to proclaim the word of God. The Church is invited to solidarity with the poor, to work for peace. And most importantly, the Church community is defined as those who "hear the poor."

A listening community know themselves as the "priesthood of believers" (1 Pet 2:5), inspired by the Spirit and their baptism to preach God's holy Word. This "preaching" involves active proclamation through words; but it also means that the preaching Church of the poor *hears* the cry of the poor (Ps 34). Listening is especially important for those who form the hierarchical Church, from Pope Francis, to the bishops, to Church commissions and presbyteries, to pastors in their community. Ivone Gebara says:

> I'd like to reinforce the idea that we are the Church too. That means getting out of a clerical or papal concept of the Church. In other words, the Church isn't just the bishops or just the Pope. They aren't the ones who deliver faith to us. They aren't the ones who give us Jesus Christ. They aren't the ones who lead us to adhere to the values that sustain life. They have a function, no doubt, but the reality of faith is inscribed in every person, then it is sustained in the community of people of faith who are able to be justice, mercy, compassion, and mutual aid in the maintenance of life for one another. Getting out of valuing hierarchical schemes and seeking collective responsibility in great and small acts is a real challenge for all of us.[1]

---

1. Gebara, interview with Lindsey, http://bilgrimage.blogspot.com/2013/08/brazilian-theologian-ivone-gebara-on.html.

Part Two: Within

Most preaching manuals deal with the "how" of the Holy Preaching: How long should the homily be? How should it be constructed? What rhetorical style should be used? What structure should be followed? Should it be written out? Text, outline, or moves?

Rhetoric *is* important. Preachers since St. Augustine and St. John Chrysostom have known of the benefits of attractive presentation for gospel proclamation. But the Fathers and Mothers considered rhetoric only a tool for the *kerygma*. The proclamation of the good news had to do primarily with *theology* and not rhetoric. Theology, in the first centuries, was the contemplation of the Holy Trinity. The Fathers and Mothers *preached* their theology—not academic discourse but, rather, an expression of the living God and the community who imaged the Holy Trinity. The proclamation was itself *theology*. Its purpose was not in the beauty of the construction and methodology—the how. The beauty was to be contemplated in the "who" of the preaching: the Holy Trinity: the *Abba* Father-Mother, the incarnate divine Person of the Son, and the Holy Spirit, the Lord and Giver of Life. The Living Three is reflected in the *community of the Holy Preaching*. In the "how," appearances are important; in the "who," *identity* is *the* primary question.

Especially important is our Christian identity, given by the Triune God when we are baptized. It is a continuing recreation and renewal in the Spirit making baptism a vibrant process throughout our lives as followers of Jesus. We become daughters and sons of the living God. Grace builds on nature (Rom 5:20), the Catholic tradition has always said. Thus, we do not receive a "new identity" so much as a confirmation of our *actual identity* as *imago Dei*. We are named, we are baptized as members into a specific culture, language and racial group, a concrete people where "there is no longer Jew or Greek, there is no longer slave or free, there is no longer male and female; for all of you are one in Christ Jesus" (Gal 3:28). The baptized receive the charism of the "Holy Preaching." Into whatever reality we are born and baptized, we become preachers, called by the sacred waters to the mission of proclamation.

The Holy Preaching

The Holy Preaching is so much broader than the Sunday twenty minutes. Jesus is incarnate in the community through the preaching, and the baptized community becomes Holy Preaching, inspired toward mission, praxis, and proclamation. The poor preaching Church are the "voice of the Spirit."[2] The Spirit preaches through the poor, and the body of Christ is manifest in the *pueblo*. I specifically refer to the Mexican immigrant community in the United States, the manifestation of Christ sent by the Holy Spirit, called by baptism, anointed to preach the gospel to the Church in the United States.[3] Although the reasons for the long and perilous journey to this country are economic, the Spirit of God has a deeper purpose—the conversion of the dominant community through the proclaiming witness of our Mexican sisters and brothers.

Identity is an important question for the Mexican immigrant.[4] It is not "I" as individual. The "who am I" is important only in regards to the question: who are *we*? By baptism, we are daughters and sons of the living God. As daughters and sons, we are sisters and brothers belonging to a holy people. José Marins relates the following story: A priest is assigned to a new parish. On his first Sunday, he preaches, "Brothers and sisters, we are sons and daughters of the living God." "Oh how beautiful," everyone says. "This is a holy priest." The second Sunday, he preaches, "If daughters and sons of the living God, we are sisters and brothers in Jesus." "Oh," the people say, "what a wonderful pastor this is going to be—so centered, so holy." The third Sunday, he says, "If we are daughters and sons of the living God and sisters and brothers in Jesus, then . . . we must all be *equal sharers* of the earth's riches." The people respond, "This new priest is too radical for us. We are going to ask the bishop for a replacement"! Marins observes that the

---

2. Comblin, *La Vida* and *The Holy Spirit and Liberation*. Rondet, *La Trinidad Narrada*, 103.

3. Montes Lara, *The Indigenous Face of God*. I am indebted to my longtime friend and colleague for her creative insights regarding the Mexican immigrant community and the sacrament of baptism.

4. Groody and Campese, *A Promised Land*, 112.

Part Two: Within

Fatherhood of God has a precise meaning in poor communities that touches the roots of the system that causes poverty. God, our Father and Mother, has a special love for the poor immigrant lacking proper documentation. If God is our Father and our Mother, and we are brothers and sisters, does not the earth equally belong to all people without regard for borders?

North Americans generally fall into two schools of thought on immigration. The conservatives say to Mexican migrants: "Go home. You do not belong here." They desire a border heavily guarded and militarized. The liberals say, "Please stay, those of you who are already here, but we need to be careful that not too many more come . . . and while we're at it, let's make those already here citizens." Both approaches are wrong, for both impose a false identity—the first turns the Mexican migrant into a non-person; the second wants an immigrant "like us and not different," part of the great American melting pot and anti-Trinitarian at core.

Gustavo Gutiérrez, OP, identifies immigrants as a large and new class of the poor. He says that the dominant community must express solidarity with the migrant by making God's option for the poor their own.[5] The migrant global poor, Gutiérrez maintains, are like Lazarus at the door of the rich man (Luke 16:19–31). The hope of migrant Lazarus is the resurrection of Jesus, not a "miracle" but, instead, the deepest meaning of life.[6] What to do when a whole people is denied *life*? What to do when their identity is negated through deportation or integration? Does the dominant community in the United States really *listen* to the voice of the Spirit through the Holy Preaching of the Mexican immigrant community?

There are three stages, I believe, in the *listening*: first, from sound to Word. Our lives are filled with noise, which tells us we are busy, constantly moving, never still and silent. Technology makes daily pace unimaginably difficult for many. I am not advocating a Luddite return to the Stone Age. However, the pace we maintain is too hectic. We only hear noise—gun violence in our cities,

---

5. Ibid., 76–86.
6. Ibid., 81.

The Holy Preaching

meaningless chatter in the work place, the grind of urban noise, the ring-tones of our cell phones—all obtrusive sounds. This leaves little possibility of listening to the Word—poetry, literature, music, the Scriptures, the voice of one another in intimate conversation, the voice of the Spirit in the words of the poor. How to simply slow down and *listen*? Even in our churches, we only want sound—any kind of sound. Brash, loud music occupies a central place in the dominant halls of worship, filling us with noise. The words are often trite, the melodies banal. This is needed, it is thought, to "keep the young people in church." Youth movements for teens in the Catholic Church in the United States are part of the "with it" parish and often develop a non-critical approach to life and society inviting little reflection. Sermons are even worse. Sensationalism replaces nourishment like a steady diet of junk food, which, if continually ingested, damages health beyond repair. It is urgent to return to the Word. Mere sounds can no longer be tolerated in our Church communities:

> The church . . . knows itself to be the hearer of the gospel. If it knows itself properly it will have no illusions about itself. It will know that it is constantly in the position of the hearer and that it will desire and have to hear ever and again. It will know that such speaking and hearing cannot be taken for granted. It will know itself to be the company of those who are always sinners who live from the concrete present-tense proclamation (*simil justus et peccator*). It will know that it cannot live today on yesterday's gospel. It must hear again and again and assembles so as to hear, and takes what steps it can to guarantee that it will indeed hear the gospel.[7]

Second, from magic to Sacrament: Some years ago, Juan Luis Segundo, SJ, wrote about the urgent need to move away from the magical view of the sacraments that often predominates in Catholic communities. Traditional Catholic sacramental theology relies on *ex opere operato* with its stress on the proper gestures and words for the efficacy of the sacrament. But when Jesus performs the

---

7. Forde, *Theology is for Proclamation*, 188.

Part Two: Within

miraculous signs in the gospels, Segundo says, he combines ritual gestures and words with *faith*, absolutely indispensable to the proper ministry and reception of the sacrament. Segundo stresses that Jesus could do no miraculous sign without the accompanying faith of the people. If the sacrament is rote ritual and words devoid of faith, it deteriorates into magic and can become a fetish. This is the one great dangers of the traditional Catholic view of the sacraments, says Segundo.[8] But ritual words and gestures, along with profound faith that "moves mountains" (Mark 11:23), give new meaning to the sacraments: magic to sacrament, founded in the experience of the Triune God and the poor preaching Church. For the Holy Preaching, emphasis is no longer given to "magic words" spoken by a solitary figure from a high pulpit every Sunday and "how" this should happen, but the "who"—the voice of the Holy Spirit in the poor, Jesus Christ walking among the people, the pueblo as Holy Preaching.[9]

Third, from club to Community: the usual Catholic parish in the United States is organized into groups. These groups vary, from ministerial associations such as Eucharistic Ministers and Proclaimers of the Word, to the Knights of Columbus, the Legion of Mary, Life Teen, Charismatic Renewal, and many others. Groups are necessary to any organization, including the Church. But they tend to stress the institutional Church in its organization, so that parish is primarily not a *community* but an institution. This happens on a larger scale in the diocese. There are certainly Protestant and Orthodox equivalents; the reader from these traditions may substitute the necessary structures. Consequently, parish and diocesan structure take on aspects of societal clubs rather than *communities* of people. Traditional Sunday preaching is often directed exclusively toward these groups. The Holy Preaching moves *emphatically* away from this structure, which is why base ecclesial communities or their equivalent become so important in the poor

---

8. Segundo, *The Sacraments Today*, 21–27. Pastro, *Enflamed*, 60–61.

9. Juan Carlos Scannone, SJ, a mentor of Pope Francis, says that phenomenology helps greatly in the move from the "magical view of life." Scannone, *Religión y Nuevo Pensamiento*, 35–76.

The Holy Preaching

preaching Church. Pope Francis' words, "How I long for a poor Church of the poor" can also be, "How I long for a Church community of *people*" (not groups!). A club works fine in society. But only an ecclesial community can serve the poor preaching Church in the contemporary world.

When the identity of the Holy Preaching is the "who," centered in the Spirit, the voice of the poor, it becomes an indispensable source of strength for the preaching Church:

> Likewise the Spirit helps us in our weakness; for we do not know how to pray as we ought, but that very Spirit intercedes with sighs too deep for words. And God, who searches the heart, knows what is the mind of the Spirit, because the Spirit intercedes for the saints according to the will of God (Rom 8:26–27).

Chapter 9

The Our Father

The Our Father is the prayer of the poor preaching Church *par excellence*. Leonardo Boff classifies it as the most important prayer of the disciple, precisely because these are the original words of Jesus.[1] Boff summarizes what praying the Our Father does for the follower of Jesus:

> The reality encompassed in the Lord's Prayer is not a pretty picture but one of heavy conflict. Here the kingdom of God confronts the kingdom of Satan. The Father is near (he is our Father) but he is also remote (in heaven). Blasphemies are spoken in this world, which imposes on us the duty to sanctify God's name. The world is ruled by all sorts of evils that exacerbate our longing for the coming of God's kingdom, which is one of justice, love, and peace. The will of God is being violated, and we must give it concrete expression in our conduct. We pray for daily bread because there are many who do not have it. We ask that God forgive us our violations of fellowship, so that we can forgive those who have offended us. We pray for strength in temptations, because otherwise we would fail miserably. We cry out to be set free from evil, because otherwise we would turn our backs on the faith forever. And in the midst of all this conflict the Lord's

---

1. Boff, *Christianity in a Nutshell*, 60–75.

The Our Father

> Prayer preserves an aura of joyful confidence and serene commitment, inasmuch as all of this is integrated into our encounter with the Father.[2]

The Our Father is sacred for those who follow Jesus because it is the only prayer we have that comes directly from the mouth of Jesus. In the early Church, it was so sacred that it formed part of the "hidden discipline," the *disciplina arcani* that the believing community kept secret lest it fall into the hands of unbelievers. The Our Father was therefore only taught once one had been initiated into the Christian community through Baptism, Confirmation, and the Eucharist.[3] Perhaps this was why many early Christian writers like St. Ambrose called the Our Father "the pearl of great price."[4] All of the teachings of Jesus are contained in the Our Father. Though the individual in private devotion prayed the Our Father, it was, more importantly, used communally, most often in the context of the liturgy.[5] The communal dimension was interpreted cosmically:

> [T]he (Our Father) covered every conceivable action of Christian life and thought, and . . . it even had much to suggest about the nature of the cosmos . . . scholars noted that the prayer was primarily a communal prayer, because of its regular use of words like 'our' or 'us.' Therefore, even though early Christians were encouraged to prayer the (Our Father) in their own devotional practices, the prayer was understood primarily to be concerned with the needs of community.[6]

The Our Father tells us about how Jesus related to the *Abba*-Father. It tells us much about the Triune God; for Jesus directs himself to *Abba* intimately—"Papa"—and is the dearly beloved Son inviting disciples to live in the Spirit of the reign of God. Joachim Jeremias points out that in one of the textual variants for

---

2. Boff, *The Lord's Prayer*, 5–6.
3. Boff, *Christianity in a Nutshell*, 67.
4. Hammerling, *The Lord's Prayer*, 3.
5. Jeremias, *The Lord's Prayer*, 2.
6. Hammerling, *The Lord's Prayer*, 124.

Part Two: Within

Luke's gospel (Luke 11:2) from the second century attested to by writers such as Sts. Gregory of Nyssa and Maximus the Confessor, the Holy Spirit is explicitly mentioned: "The Holy Spirit come upon us and cleanse us."[7] The Father, whose name is holy, is "in heaven," yet "our *Abba*" is concerned about our "daily bread" and our preservation us from the "evil one." The Our Father reminds the follower of Jesus that God is more intimate to us than we can imagine. It is most important, if we are God's beloved daughters and sons, to treat one another, and the entire cosmos, as sister and brother—simply because God is our *Abba*. If we love the way that *Abba* God does, if we seek justice, assuring that the poor have their daily bread, if we forgive as we are forgiven, then surely the reign of God is at hand—a reality in which we hope.

The Our Father is the basic prayer of the Christian. Many have dedicated devotional tracts and sermons to it, including Karl Barth, Joachim Jeremias, Gerhard Ebeling, N.T. Wright, Dietrich Bonhoeffer, and Leonardo Boff. It is among the most cherished of all Christian prayers. Can the Our Father be used as a summary for what the preaching Church of the poor is called to? Can it be *Magna Carta* for the community of the Holy Preaching? As we pray for the reign of God and live in its hope, how do we see it? Ethereal "other-world" illusion or solidly present in anticipated hope, right here, right now, in our community, in solidarity with the poor, in our beloved Mother Earth, in our cosmos?[8]

Preaching is a charism conferred on every believer at baptism, and the Our Father is a prayer specifically related to baptism.[9] It was reserved for the baptized and only prayed by them. What if we returned to the *disciplina arcani* regarding the Our Father? What if it were prayed earnestly by the preaching Church and those in solidarity with the poor? The Our Father summarized the early Christian *kerygma*. Every word, phrase, and petition of the Our Father gives identity to the poor preaching Church.

---

7. Jeremias, *The Lord's Prayer*, 2–3.
8. Green, *Bonhoeffer Reader*, 340–51.
9. Jeremias, *The Lord's Prayer*, 3.

The Our Father

The following meditation on the Our Father is offered, then, for the Holy Preaching, for all who strive to proclaim the good news to the poor, called to be a "poor Church for the poor" in the now famous words of Pope Francis.

"Our Father"

The gospels contain two versions of the Our Father, Luke 11:2–4 and Matt 6:9–13. The *Didache* and other ancient sources also attest to the Our Father, adding the doxology ("for Yours is the kingdom and the power and the glory forever, Amen"). Jeremias says that the Lucan version is probably the original, but Matthew is perhaps closer to the intentionality of Jesus. The Our Father gives an Oriental worldview of the meaning of "father"—"merciful and gracious" *Abba*. The word, Jeremias says, "as applied to God, thus encompasses, from earliest times, something of what the word 'mother' signifies among us."[10] When we pray the Our Father, then, we pray to God, our Father and our *Mother*. Manuel Arias Montes, a Mexican indigenous theologian and pastor from the *Mixteca Alta* culture in Oaxaca, prays to God "Father and Mother" in all liturgical prayers he offers with the people. The Our Father is directed to a tender, merciful, compassionate *Abba* God who loves with the tender mercies of a Mother and a Father:

> Jesus . . . viewed this filial form of address for God as the heart of that revelation which had been granted him by the Father. In this term *abba* the ultimate mystery of his mission and his authority is expressed. He, to whom the Father had granted full knowledge of God, has the messianic prerogative of addressing him with the familiar address of a son. This term *abba* is an *ipsissima vox* of Jesus and contains *in nuce* his message and his claim to have been sent from the Father.[11]

---

10. Ibid., 17–18.
11. Ibid., 20.

Part Two: Within

In the Our Father, we do not pray to "my Father." *Abba* God is kind, compassionate, tender, and merciful toward a *people*. The Our Father is not primarily an individual prayer; the texts from the first centuries are *communal*. Prayer in the early Church was always communal. This was particularly true of the Eucharist; and it is true of liturgical prayer in the preaching Church *today*. The "our" is most especially remembered in the communities of the poor.

"Who Art in Heaven"

After our talk about the Our Father directed to a concrete people awaiting the fulfillment of the reign of God for the poor, for the earth, for the cosmos . . . are we now to think of the God in heaven through "pie in the sky" eyes with little reference to *reality* experienced by the poor? If this were the meaning of "who art in heaven," we would be truly unfortunate. Jesus promises "life in abundance" (John 10:10), and he means life that begins *here* and *now*. In the great Mystery that is God, life is eternal and never ends; but this life in Jesus begins *now*. We don't just "wait for it to happen" at an undisclosed future time. Eschatology means this and only this: in the words of the old African-American spiritual, "keep your eyes on the prize, hold on." The prize is the concrete justice of God for the poor and the *anawim* now, not in some distant future. Eschatology is more about *hope* than faith. "Who art in heaven" can only mean one thing: that our God who is infinitely tender and compassionate is also infinitely *Other*. But this One who is "infinitely Other" is infinitely *close* in the Incarnation. God becomes flesh in Jesus, in our culture, our poverty, our language, our life, our world, our cosmos. The God who is "in heaven" is the God who is enfleshed, impoverished, emptied "for us and for our salvation."

The Our Father

"Hallowed Be Thy Name"

For our Jewish ancestors in the faith, and for our Jewish sisters and brothers today, the name of God is so sacred that it cannot even be uttered; it behooves us to have the same profound respect for the name of God. If we nurture dignity for God's name, the God who is *Abba* Father and Mother, we will reverence sisters and brothers who are daughters and sons of the same *Abba*. We will especially respect the poorest and the most oppressed. Hallowing God's holy name is respecting the poor and the cosmos.

We use the word "God" so carelessly that often we speak not of the true God at all but an idol. Jon Sobrino and Latin American theologians remind us that the real faith problem in the contemporary world is not atheism; rather, it is idolatry—placing an illusory god before the one true God. If God is illusory, everything is illusory—including the poor. What is worse, the poor are not only illusory but *invisible*. In Exod 3:14, God gives the sacred name, "I Am Who I Am." This name has little to do with metaphysics and everything to do with what God *does*, how God *acts*: with justice for the poor. It is, in short, the *praxis of God* that makes God's name holy, unutterable. In Latin American theology this passage is central because God's identity, expressed in the Sacred Tetragrammaton, is intimately related to how God acts. God's very name is hallowed through God's actions. We then understand that the daughters and sons of the *Abba* God, whose name is sanctified through divine action, are also deeply worthy of respect, honor, and dignity.

There is yet another aspect to the holiness of God's name. Gerhard Lohfink says that in the Scriptures, God makes God's own name holy by calling together a *holy people*, by choosing a people to be God's own. Jesus Christ is the definitive Word of this gathering:

> "Sanctify your name"—this means, in other words, nothing other than "Gather and renew your people! Let it become anew the true people of God!" Jesus was obviously convinced that this eschatological gathering of

the people by God had already begun *now*, just as the coming of the kingdom was *now* taking place. And Jesus was convinced that the gathering of the people and the coming of the kingdom were occurring *through him*.[12]

"Thy Kingdom Come"

This is the central point of the Our Father, what Leonardo Boff calls "the very heart of the Lord's prayer."[13] All of Jesus' actions, his compassion, his healings, his preaching, his being, revolve around the reign of God. This reign is not "other-worldly." Dietrich Bonhoeffer considered the reign of God something very earthly indeed! In a lecture of November 1932, he refers to the concrete nature and reality of God's reign. God's world, he says, is *our* world.[14] N. T. Wright echoes the sentiments of Bonhoeffer:

> The second main petition in the Lord's Prayer—"Thy Kingdom Come"—rules out any idea that the Kingdom of God is a purely heavenly (that is, 'other-worldly') reality. Thy kingdom come, we pray, thy will be done, *on earth as it is in heaven*. 'Heaven' and 'earth' are the two interlocking arenas of God's good world . . . Think of the vision at the end of Revelation. It isn't about humans being snatched up from earth to heaven. The holy city, the new Jerusalem, comes down *from* heaven to earth. God's space and ours are finally married, integrated at last. That is what we pray for when we pray "thy Kingdom come."[15]

The reign of God is the center of the *prayer* of the preaching Church because it is the center of the *praxis* of the preaching Church. Prayer leads to praxis, praxis to prayer. Gustavo Gutiérrez defines theology as "a critical reflection on praxis in the light of the word of God." Theology is contemplation of the Triune God, so prayer and praxis are intimately related. Bonhoeffer reminds us

12. Lohfink, *Jesus and Community*, 16.
13. Boff, *The Lord's Prayer*, 54.
14. DBW 12:264–78.
15. Wright, *The Lord and His Prayer*, 24–25.

The Our Father

of the unity of "prayer and action for justice," writing from prison that these are two hallmarks of the Christian life most important in the following of Jesus today.[16]

"Thy Will Be Done on Earth as It is in Heaven"

What would it look like if God's will were perfectly done "on earth as in heaven"? Perhaps this answers the problem of theodicy, which turns the will of God into magic. "Why is there suffering in the world if God is good?" is the classical expression of the question. According to the Our Father, theodicy is the wrong question. We pray that God's will be *perfectly* done "on earth *as in heaven*"— which assumes that the plan of God is frustrated by human evil. Remember Flip Wilson's "the devil made me do it"? The story is as ancient as creation and the fall. Adam blames Eve, and Eve blames the serpent, it has been said. We always make someone *else* responsible for sin. But humanity is responsible for injustice—to the poor and the cosmos. Human beings are responsible for evil in the world. When Pope Francis speaks of human responsibility for global warming in *Laudato Si*, he quotes Patriarch Bartholomew:

> Patriarch Bartholomew has spoken in particular of the need for each of us to repent of the ways we have harmed the planet, for "inasmuch as we all generate small ecological damage," we are called to acknowledge "our contribution, smaller or greater, to the disfigurement and destruction of creation." He has repeatedly stated this firmly and persuasively, challenging us to acknowledge our sins against creation: "For human beings . . . to destroy the biological diversity of God's creation; for human beings to degrade the integrity of the earth by causing changes in its climate, by stripping the earth of its natural forests or destroying its wetlands; for human beings to contaminate the earth's waters, its land, its air, and its life—these are sins." For "to commit a crime

---

16. Green, *Bonhoeffer Reader*, 788.

against the natural world is a sin against ourselves and a sin against God."[17]

In the Lord's Prayer, we pray that God's will be done on earth perfectly as it is in heaven. When Jesus says, "Be perfect, therefore, as your heavenly Father is perfect" (Matt 5:48), he does not refer to an impossible task, an "ideal," as has often been said of the Beatitudes in Christian piety. Jesus is placing an *evangelical demand* on his followers. God's will in the world is not an abstract ideal. It is done perfectly as consequence of faithful daily discipleship. When the preaching Church of the poor prays that God's will be done, they act in union with God's will—the Holy Preaching lives as the *Holy Preaching*.

"Give Us This Day Our Daily Bread"

When Pope John Paul II came to Perú in 1985, he visited a *pueblo jóven* ("young town") in the *conosur* (south cone) of Lima called Villa El Salvador, named for Jesus the Savior. The *pueblos jóvenes* of Lima are desperately poor areas of the city recently settled by those who migrate from the mountainous areas of Perú looking for a better life. The people would organize *invaciones*—"invasions" of unpopulated areas around the city belonging to the government or empty land in private sectors. I worked as a young priest in the *pueblo jóven* just north of Villa El Salvador called Pamplona Alta. The parish organized a *peregrinaje* (pilgrimage) to Villa El Salvador. We left at four in the morning and processed the seven miles south, arriving some hours later at the place in Villa El Salvador where the papal Mass was to be celebrated. There were over one million people gathered—all poor—and that day they were the poor preaching Church, the Holy Preaching. One group carried a large sign with the words: *Santo Padre, tenemos hambre, queremos pan*—"Holy Father, we are hungry, we want bread." John Paul put his prepared homily aside and addressed himself, as pastor, to the poor. But it was really the poor, through the simple words on the

17. Pope Francis, *Laudato Si*, paragraph 8.

sign, who became the Holy Preaching that day. John Paul based his words on "give us this day our daily bread," saying Jesus meant these words literally, and it was a "sin crying out to the heavens" that there were people who did not have their daily bread and were physically hungry. This petition of the Our Father is prayed on behalf of the poor *by* the poor, and it is *the* prayer of the preaching Church.

"Forgive Us Our Trespasses as We Forgive Those Who Trespass Against Us"

The meaning of this petition is simple and obvious. We pray to be forgiven to the extent that we *forgive*. Karl Barth puts it bluntly—how do we dare not forgive one another when we stand *bankrupt* before God?

> [I]f we reflect upon this forgiveness which we must grant to others, how much more we feel that we must pray. For, if we refuse to make this small gesture, we are far from having laid hold of the divine forgiveness. . . . [W]e confess our bankruptcy; and if we are unwilling to do so, we must give up asking God's forgiveness. We must recognize that our own cause is lost, and if we do, it becomes for us a victorious cause, for it is then in the hands of him who has forgiven and who still forgives.[18]

A Church community that does not forgive cannot be the Holy Preaching.

"Lead Us Not Into Temptation but Deliver Us from Evil"

This last petition of the Lord's Prayer is integrally connected with what goes before, particularly the will of God, which is always perfect and good. We pray for the grace to do the will of God perfectly, to not act in conjunction with the Evil One. When we are tested,

---

18. Barth, *Prayer*, 59.

tempted, we are presented with a choice: between good and evil, perfection and imperfection, and the infinite shades of grey that stand between the two poles. We remember the wisdom of Dietrich Bonhoeffer, who says that ethical action at times means choosing what is "evil" so that God's will is done perfectly. The real ethical question for Bonhoeffer is not the choice between good and evil; rather, it is asking the question: what is God's will?[19] God's will, as Bonhoeffer reminds us from prison, lies deeply hidden beneath millions of possibilities.[20] When we ask to be delivered from evil, we are praying that God's will be done perfectly.

The Our Father is the prayer of the preaching Church of the poor and those in solidarity with them. The "Amen" at the end summarizes the Holy Preaching: So be it.

---

19. *DBWE* 6:47
20. *DBWE* 8:515

Chapter 10

The Holy Spirit
Voice of the Preaching Church

St. Irenaeus speaks of the God with two hands—Jesus and the Holy Spirit. It is a rich image of the Holy Trinity. Hands symbolize doing, *acting*. José Comblin says that these two hands are the "action" of the Triune God.[1] The mediating Word and Sacrament Jesus Christ is the incarnate hand that concretely touches the life of the Church community and is, in his very Person, the body of Christ, the community. The artistic, unpredictable hand of God is the Holy Spirit, who hovers over our void and nothingness to create (Gen 1:2)—*creatio ex nihilo, veni Creator Spiritus*. This hand of God is difficult to pin down but is no less active than the Son. We see the glory of the Son (John 1:14) in his humanity. But in order to *see* the action of the Holy Spirit in the Church and the world, we use *different* senses that compliment sight, hearing, smell, taste, and touch. We "discern" the hand of the Spirit in the world—a gift that "sees" on a deeper level, especially bequeathed to the Church community through St. Ignatius of Loyola and the Society of Jesus.[2]

---

1. Comblin, *Tiempo de Acción*.

2. See Rahner's *Spirit in the World* for a definitive Ignatian expression of the concrete presence of the Spirit.

Part Two: Within

The Holy Spirit cannot be "seen." But the action of the hand that is the Spirit *certainly* can. We discern the Spirit's presence in the world and testify to the presence through the Holy Preaching. Gregory Heille reminds preachers to "pay attention"—excellent advise for the discernment of the Spirit! Paying attention can be done in many ways: through Ignatian discernment, or developing a prayerful stance toward the Holy Preaching, or—simply keeping eyes and hearts open to the unpredictable Spirit! There is yet another piece of advice: do not *obstruct* the Spirit. The action of the Spirit is discerned, and room is made for the work of the Spirit. The preacher is ready to shift direction immediately at the promptings of the Spirit. The direction shifting often means simply not standing in the way of the Spirit. The preacher is always open to the work of the Spirit in the poor preaching Church. Do the words of formal liturgical preaching inspire the Holy Preaching toward action that is in union with the mission of the Spirit, or do the words of the preacher block the action of the Holy Spirit preaching through the Church community? Does the institutional Church, represented by the ordained preacher, listen to the voice of the Spirit in the poor preaching Church?

It is a challenge to discern the movement of the Spirit. Through the Incarnation, we "see" Jesus in his body; but the Spirit cannot be seen and is only discerned through his action, through her sound: "The wind blows where it chooses, and you hear the sound of it, but you do not know where it comes from or where it goes. So it is with everyone who is born of the Spirit" (John 3:8). How do we hear the sound of the Spirit in the poor preaching Church? How does the Spirit speak, sound, sing? Preacher and preaching Church "tune in" the Spirit blowing among the Church community, the poor, and creation.

The Eastern Orthodox community has often said that the Western Church gives short shrift to the work of the Spirit. That is truer than we in the West want to believe. The Holy Spirit has been called the "forgotten Person" of the Living Three. Eastern Orthodoxy has maintained the tradition and theology of the Holy Spirit more faithfully. Eastern Churches have criticized the West

The Holy Spirit

for giving God only one hand while the other is restrained. The Western Church has been called "Christomonist"—solely centered on the person and work of Christ. But so as not to enter territory many fear to tread—the *Filioque* for instance—I wonder if there is a simpler reason for the "Spirit paucity" of the West. Have we willy-nilly separated mysticism and theology into yet another dualism? Read the writings of Sts. Teresa of Avila, John of the Cross, and Catherine of Siena—just to mention a few of the great Western mystics. They are immersed in the theological language of the Spirit. It is, unfortunately, language that is not sufficiently respected by the theological academy or the institutional Church. The East often seems closer to the sources—the Scriptures, the Fathers and Mothers, the Tradition. The West has spoken of a systematic approach to the Spirit—"pneumatology" is the word often used—but the challenge is that this hand of God is . . . the Holy Spirit! As Karl Barth has said, "No one *has* the Spirit." We do not "possess" the Spirit. The Holy Spirit possesses, takes hold, of us! So how then to speak of the work of the Spirit? Perhaps the answer is not "analytical" at all; systematic theology cannot really say much about the mission of the Holy Spirit. But *symbolic* theology can.[3] Western mystics are comfortable in the realm of poetry and art. But *theology* in the West has a difficult time with *symbol*. There is an urgent need to return to the epoch in which theology—the contemplation of the Trinity—felt comfortable in the world of symbol. Mysticism and theology are of one piece.

It is important to pay attention to the voice of the Spirit in the poor. When the voice is heard, the preacher moves out of the path of the Spirit and readies the way for discerning the Spirit in the Holy Preaching. There are ways we can facilitate the work of the Spirit. They should be pursued actively so that the liturgical preacher never stands in the way of the Holy Preaching. The Spirit is so unpredictable! Spirit-people not understood by the institution are held in suspicion. How does the Holy Spirit work in the

---

3. See Brock, *The Luminous Eye*, for an excellent synopsis of the theology of St. Ephrem the Syrian. Brock says that Ephrem's theology is symbolic, done primarily through poetry and music.

Part Two: Within

people, the poor preaching Church, the Holy Preaching? Where does the Spirit inspire the poor Church community into action? Where do the poor *live* (Gustavo Gutiérrez)? How do we become a "poor Church for the poor"? Perhaps the most concrete way for the ordained preacher to look at these questions and *listen* to the voice of the Spirit in the poor preaching Church is precisely what Pope Francis has suggested: that ministers, presbyters, bishops, leave the comfort of the sacristy and go out in search of the people, so that the pastor takes on the "smell of the sheep." We are called to go to those places where we least expect to find the Spirit (*Spiritus absconditus*?)—the poor, women, those oppressed in any fashion. Is table fellowship important to the ordained preacher? It was for Jesus. It is at the table of the poor that the Holy Preaching is nurtured and the Spirit freed to work in the hearts of the poor. Why give God only one hand?

Liturgists and sacramental theologians have long made an urgent plea for a theology of the Holy Spirit. Pay attention, they tell us, to the writings of the Greek and Syrian Fathers and Mothers; pay attention to Eastern Orthodox theology. Many Western theologians have scarcely heard names like Paul Evdokimov, Alexander Schmemman, Vladimir Lossky, Nicolas Afanasiev, and Nikos Nissiotis. It will be important to "pay attention" to voices overlooked by Catholic theologies. Raimon Panikkar is a name I have already mentioned. Víctor Codina, SJ, is another, largely unknown in most Western theological academies in the Northern Hemisphere. A professor of theology in Cochabamba, Bolivia, where he has taught for many years, he is immersed in the theology of the poor and discerns the promptings of the Spirit in the *pueblo*. Shortly after finishing his doctoral studies, Codina was assigned to post-doctoral work at St. Sergius Institute in Paris, where he studied with Eastern Orthodox greats. His works stress two areas of theology in need of constant renewal: ecclesiology and pneumatology. For the discerning theologian, the two are integrally related. It is often said that Orthodox theology fosters a "living Church" because of the profound intimacy between the people and the Spirit of God. Víctor Codina senses the intimacy. I

The Holy Spirit

have included a sampling of his works in the bibliography. Codina and the Latin Americans understand that *both* hands of God work in the preaching Church to bring about the Holy Preaching.

And what of the work of the Holy Spirit in the preaching Church of the poor? How is the work of the Spirit nurtured among the *pueblo*? How do ordained preachers assure that the primary work of the Holy Preaching is not what they do as individual preachers but what the preaching Church does? What is the most important work of the pastor, the ordained preacher, in a parish community?

I am convinced that the primary work of the pastor is *formation*. I use the word with hesitancy. In *Ethics*, Dietrich Bonhoeffer writes that there is only one "formation" in the Christian community: *conformitas*, the "conformation" of Christ to the people so that St. Paul's words to the Galatians become ours: "For through the law I died to the law, so that I might live to God. I have been crucified with Christ; and it is no longer I who live, but it is Christ who lives in me. And the life I now live in the flesh I live by faith in the Son of God, who loved me and gave himself for me" (Gal 2:19-20).[4] Christian formation involves accompanying the people in enfleshing the words of Paul into the heart of the community so that the Holy Preaching becomes the body of Christ, "Christ existing as Church community," and the Holy Spirit the voice of the poor.

Many years ago, the Medical Mission Sisters wrote a song called *Spirit of God*. The chorus sings: "Spirit of God . . . fill the earth, bring it to birth and blow . . . 'til I be but breath of the Spirit blowing in me."[5] *This* is the prayer of the preaching Church: that we become *only* breath of the Spirit in our preaching, that we embody Paul's words that Christ lives in the *pueblo*. The question for the pastor becomes then: how to accompany the body of Christ and the voice of the poor as presence of the Spirit in the world today? It will mean a radical re-prioritizing of the work of the pastor, now so dedicated to the "maintenance" of the parish. It will mean the redirection of the Church community, as many have observed,

---

4. *DBWE* 6:76–103.
5. http://www.youtube.com/watch?v=_EYMoTyVWYI.

Part Two: Within

from maintenance to mission: a mission whose only purpose is to enable the people to be the living Christ, the breath of the Spirit, the two hands of God embracing the world God so loves (John 3:16).

The work of the Holy Spirit is a creative work. God creates with both hands. *Veni Creator Spiritus* . . . The work of creation is often accredited only to God Father-Mother. But in the Christian tradition, creation is the work of the Triune God. Killian McDonnell suggests that we have not even begun to look at the work of the Spirit in the Scriptures. If we were to develop a scriptural theology of the Holy Spirit, there is, McDonnell asserts, copious material as yet untapped by Western theologians. One of the best places to begin is the story of creation, specifically, the work of the Spirit in Genesis: "In the beginning when God created the heavens and the earth, the earth was a formless void and darkness covered the face of the deep, while a wind (*ruah, pneuma,* Spirit) from God swept over the face of the waters. Then God said, 'Let there be light'; and there was light" (Gen 1:1–3). In the beginning, there is chaos, darkness, formlessness, void. But the Spirit of God "hovers" over the waters. God's wind, the *Ruah*-Spirit, is present from the very beginning, like the Logos, the Dabar *YHWH*: "And God said . . ." God creates with wind-Spirit and *Logos*-speaking. The *Logos* and the Spirit are the two creative hands of God. It is not only the First of the Divine Three who creates—which is why we must be careful when looking for inclusive ways to speak of the Trinity. My first attempt at an inclusive sign of the cross was heretical: "In the name of the Creator, and of the Redeemer, and of the One who sanctifies"—modalism, I fear! Rather, the work of creation, salvation, and sanctification belongs to each Person in turn. The First Person shares the creative activity with the two hands, the Son and the Spirit. The Father cannot do the work of creation alone; it is a community effort. I still use inclusive Trinitarian language when I preach and pray with people sensitive to the exclusive language inherent in our Trinitarian theology. But in fidelity to the Tradition, it is important to maintain the distinctive role of each Person: "In the name of God, Father and Mother, in the name of Jesus, Son

The Holy Spirit

and Brother, and in the name of the Spirit of life and love. Amen." Or in the Augustinian tradition (rightly criticized by some Eastern Orthodox theologians): "In the name of the One Who Loves, the One Who Is Beloved, and the One Who is Love. Amen." The work of creation is the work of the Holy Trinity. The Spirit's role is the divine wind that "blows where she will." We can only see—or hear—the effects in the Holy Preaching.

Does the creative work of the Spirit have a *special* role in the Holy Preaching? How often have we preachers started from absolutely nothing? Usually every week! Even after the work of prayer and study is over, I find that I am usually unable to articulate what *exactly* I think I have heard. Most ordained preachers have had the experience of writing out their weekend preaching . . . and then having it "mysteriously changed" by the creative work of the Spirit. I am not arguing for careless preaching. We have all heard preachers who are unprepared and rely on the "Spirit" for the words. The preacher tempts God, as we used to say. It never works. Good preaching is fired in the crucible of prayer, reflection, study, and paying attention. However, I often find that after doing the work of prayer, study, and writing, the Spirit steps in at the moment of preaching and totally *surprises* me. Each preaching community is gathered by the Spirit, different from day-to-day, hour-to-hour, moment-to-moment. The Sunday preacher must make way for the creative work of the Holy Preaching—the Spirit in the *community* that preaches, the preaching Church. God moves there, among God's holy people, and it is the work of the ordained preacher to *listen* to the Spirit speaking through the people in the very act of preaching. Preaching is a creative work never belonging solely to the ordained preacher but always to the Spirit and the preaching Church in dialogue with the preacher. That is why African-American preaching is so powerful in its "call—response" methodology. The people become the preacher, the preacher becomes the people, and the Spirit transforms both into a preaching Church. The pastor, who normally preaches on Sundays, must give priority time to the Holy Preaching, but Dietrich Bonhoeffer taught his students in Finkenwalde that all aspects of ministry are, strictly speaking, *preaching* ministries.[6]

Perhaps, then, the priority of the pastor is no longer facilities or maintenance of traditional groups like the Knights of Columbus. The pastor searches out the poor so that they become the center of community life and the preaching Church within the parish. Formation becomes the new priority of the mission Church, formation that helps the poor know they are the body of Christ and the breath of the Spirit. The breath of the Spirit becomes the Word in the poor, the *real* evangelizers who preach the gospel to the wealthy. The pastor "pays attention" to the poor; *that* is the priority. We share what was freely given to us: the message of the gospel. This searching out the poor in the community—present in most every parish—will manifest itself in the way the pastor preaches on Sunday morning because the poor and their suffering will be brought into the pulpit. The pastor will devote the necessary time during the week to providing quality formation programs that enable the poor to become, by the *epiclesis* of the Spirit, the Holy Preaching . . . the people of God, the body of Christ, and the creation of the Holy Spirit.

Formation of the poor preaching Church is a two-pronged effort: first, the Sunday preaching must be given priority emphasis—not parish finances, maintenance of the facilities, or catering to the "dominant" community. All these things form part of the ministry of the pastor. But effort cannot be exclusively there, and these tasks should never eclipse the work of the Holy Preaching. Pope Francis has written that quality time *must* be devoted to the Sunday preaching in prayer, reflection, and study.[7] The Sunday preaching's *sole* function is to enliven the preaching Church to do the *real* preaching. I will devote no space here to actual methodology for preparing the Sunday homily. But there are many resources available to pastors, and they should be used. I direct words of encouragement particularly to us Catholic pastors, who have given scant attention to the Word, justifying the lack by saying we are a

6. *DBWE* 14:560.
7. *Evangelii Gaudium*, 145–159.

The Holy Spirit

"sacramental Church"—to the detriment of Word *and* Sacrament! Protestants have always affirmed the importance of the Word. But even they should reflect on the creative work of the Spirit in the preaching Church—the Spirit does not restrict herself to "God's word" for an hour on Sunday mornings! And though Orthodox communities have maintained the tradition of the Holy Spirit better, they, too, should pay close attention to the Holy Preaching.

Second, formation of the poor preaching Church into the body of Christ and the breath of the Spirit means accompanying them as they find their voice; not *being* their voice, but *enlivening them* to be the voice of the Spirit. This means adult education takes on an importance that it has rarely been given. Again, the priority here is to search out the poor and to make them the primary beneficiaries of the study and prayer of the pastor. Pastors know this is not difficult, even in wealthy parishes. First-world countries, including the geographic areas that were exclusively the domain of the rich, are quickly becoming places of the poor as well. But even where that is not true, the pastor of a wealthy parish can "form" (remember *conformitas*!) the rich so that they are in solidarity with the poor. If you are a pastor, ask yourself: how much time do I dedicate to the poor? Usually, if we answer honestly . . . not much. A concrete way this can happen is through the Sunday preaching and adult formation programs—quality programs that receive the attention they deserve from the pastor. If a pastor does not feel qualified, there are other possibilities available. City parishes often can take advantage of schools of theology or universities. There are other experts in the preaching Church we pastors often overlook—formation programs in neighboring parishes and beyond—to which people can be sent for quality formation in the Holy Preaching. The people deserve formation in fundamental theology—with a special eye toward Scripture. People thirst for knowledge of the living God (John 17:3). Or do we make a liar of the psalmist: "My soul is thirsting for the living God, when shall I see God face to face" (Ps 42)?

Preaching and adult education *can* become priority for pastors. But priorities must be rearranged. The pastor must assure that the divine wind blow until the preaching Church is "but breath of the Spirit"—and not only regarding "formation of the people." Remember: *you* are responsible for staying updated in theology and ministry. That does not happen magically but is the result of *discipline*. Time must be set aside for the preparation of preaching, for keeping abreast of theological and ministerial studies, for the preparation of a solid programs of adult formation—*conformitas*—directed toward formation of, and solidarity with, the poor. It is the creative work of the Spirit of God. *Veni Sancte Spiritus*, come Holy Spirit. Every pastor, every preaching community, the Holy Preaching, the preaching Church of the poor, should make the Pentecost sequence a regular prayer. For it is the creative Spirit who always comes when and where least expected. The wind blows especially among the poor, for the sequence reminds us that the Spirit is *Pater pauperum*, the Father of the Poor.

Part Three

AMONG

"Preaching does not save us, but practices do."[1]

Praxis is Christian discipleship and practice. Nothing better defines the people of God. Action requires community, and community means "among." The preposition implies "together" in community as *pueblo*. "Among" is our primary condition as human beings. We are never alone, even when we are solitary. The *Sacra Praedicatio*, as first envisioned by Dominic, was more than simple word. It was *community* of women and men living "among," together, proclaiming the good news, living it in praxis-discipleship. The Word of the Holy Preaching, lived in the praxis community of the "among," is directed toward *action*, a way of living in which praxis is preaching, and preaching, in turn, inspires praxis. The preaching Church "among" the poor is the community dedicated to following the poor Jesus. Preaching and praxis-discipleship are integral part of the community of the Holy Preaching experienced in the "among." More than "result" of the Sunday preaching (for traditional preaching is often defined by results), praxis arising from the Holy Preaching is actually *part* of the preaching event

1. Boff, *Christianity in a Nutshell*, 67.

Part Three: Among

itself. I have often said that preaching can no longer be defined by what the individual preacher *does* every Sunday morning. The only adequate definition of preaching is found in the *community*, the "among" of the people of God. Preacher and *community* both participate, speaking and listening, in the "among," *as* the preaching Church of the poor. The universal Church has the obligation to listen earnestly to the poor and their gospel proclamation. Thus the Church community moves towards the praxis of solidarity with the poor in faithful discipleship, in proclamation of the good news to the poor, in the community of the Holy Preaching "living-among."

Chapter 11

The Preaching Mexican Immigrant Community in the United States

On December 18, 2013, a group of about fifty gathered in the main town square of Kent, WA, to pray. The prayer was based around two Scripture readings: Lev 19:33–34 and Matt 25:31–40. Leviticus uses the Hebrew word *ger*, traditionally translated alien, stranger, or foreigner in English. The translations are misleading. Immigrant or migrant is perhaps a more accurate translation.[1] Even the New Revised Standard Version uses "alien"—the word the dominant community in the United States uses to describe undocumented Mexican immigrants ("illegal alien"). It is considered pejorative by the *pueblo*, first, because people are never illegal but, rather, equal in dignity before God; and second, because people are not aliens but human beings. Listen to the passage when *ger* is translated "migrant": "When a *migrant* resides with you in your land, you shall not oppress the *migrant*. The *migrant* who resides with you shall be to you as the citizen among you; you shall love the *migrant* as yourself, for you were *migrants* in the land of Egypt: I am the Lord your God." This was the version we used in the Kent Town Plaza prayer vigil.

---

1. See Pastro, *Enflamed*, 42–45.

Part Three: Among

In Matthew 25, Christ says the following: "I was a stranger (immigrant, migrant) and you welcomed me . . . truly I tell you, just as you did it to one of the least of these who are members of my family, you did it to me." All present, English and Spanish-speaking parishioners as well as those passing by, were invited to reflect on the *migrant* among us. The migrant should not be oppressed, but rather treated as a fellow citizen. The migrant is to be loved as we love ourselves: "You shall love the Lord your God with all your heart, and with all your soul, and with all your strength, and with all your mind; and your neighbor as yourself" (Luke 10:27).

The vigil was organized by Holy Spirit Parish through the inspiration of a Mexican man prominent in the business community, himself a naturalized citizen of the United States, who has been here with his family for many years. He came to me several months prior to the prayer vigil with a simple request: what can the Church community do to stop the hemorrhaging of people from their adopted home? He spoke of his meditation that morning, a reflection on Moses' confrontation of Pharaoh: "The Lord God says, 'Let my people go'" (Exod 9:1). But he could only hear the words, "Let my people *stay*." We both agreed a prayer service for December 18—the United Nations "Day of the Migrant"—would be appropriate. Pope Francis had just written a pastoral letter on migration (*Message for the Migrants and Refugees*, September 24, 2013) directed to immigrants and those who worked with them. We especially wanted to draw attention to "Let my people *stay*"—the question of deportation—and to meet and pray in a public forum. The majority of the fifty people present were Mexican immigrants from the six base ecclesial communities of the parish. But there were also some English-speaking parishioners in solidarity. The poor preaching Church gathered in prayer proclaimed to Pharaoh, in the tradition of Moses, that people have a *right* to immigrate, a natural right irrevocably supported in Scripture and Church documents.

"Let my people *stay*." In recent years, despite the talk of immigration reform, the number of deportations of undocumented immigrants is at record highs—some four hundred thousand every year.[2] Some present at the prayer service had relatives and friends that had been deported with little opportunity to return. Deportees leave husbands, wives, children, family, friends, and work behind. It is not uncommon for someone who has been in the United States for years to be deported. When an undocumented immigrant is detained—often just for a traffic violation—there is little recourse to legal counsel. They are shipped to the nearest immigration detention facility—in the case of Kent, the facility in Fife fifteen miles to the south—and stay there until they are finally deported. And usually they *are* deported. In one recent case, an active young couple in the parish with two children were separated after immigration authorities detained the father at his work place. After the woman and children waited desperately for several months (the husband was the primary salary source for the family), he was finally "returned" to Mexico. She and the children waited another several months before returning themselves.

This unchecked deportation poignantly points to the deeper issue of immigration reform—a serious question Pope Francis has called attention to time and again. His first official journey outside the Vatican was to visit the island of Lampedusa in July of 2013. Lampedusa is a first port of call for immigrants, mostly undocumented, from Africa to Europe. They set out on fishing boats, overcrowded and overloaded into tiny boats and thus chronically susceptible to the Mediterranean storms that are common in the waters between the African coast and Lampedusa. Pope Francis, after reading the newspaper account of a tragedy in which three-hundred immigrants died in transit, made the spontaneous decision to accompany them. He flew from Rome, unprepared and on the regular airline, to Lampedusa. The Eucharist was celebrated from an altar constructed from the wood of one of the sunken boats and an ambo made from the same wood. Pope Francis then said that world migration should be among the highest priorities of the human rights agenda.

---

2. http://www.nytimes.com/2013/09/24/us/immigrant-population-shows-signs-of-growth-estimates-show.html?_r=0

Part Three: Among

The United States shares its southern border with Mexico. The northern neighbor in this sharing is a First World country. But the southern neighbor, euphemistically called a "developing" economy by neo-liberal theorists, is a Third World country. This is the only place in the world where a Third World country shares a border with a First World neighbor.[3] As poverty has more and more enveloped many areas of Mexico—from Chiapas and Oaxaca to Michoacán, Guerrero, and Jalisco—people have sought refuge, a better way of life, an escape from the poverty, a way to provide for their families in Mexico, in the northern First World neighbor.

Mexican people are welcomed in the United States because of the low-paying jobs they accept that no one else will. This has been referred to as "institutionalized slavery." At the same time, Mexican immigrants are not welcome and, in fact, discouraged by the government from immigrating. They are deported when captured and discriminated against when working at labor no one else wants. Though traditionally viewed as a nation accepting the immigrant with open arms ("Give me your tired, your poor, your huddled masses..."), apparently in the case of Mexicans, or people from Central or Latin America, the opposite is true.

Mexican people have a long history in the United States. Much of the Southwest at one time belonged to Mexico and was lost during the Mexican American War. Many ancestors of people now living in the Southwest were at one time Mexican citizens.

Mexican people often immigrate to the United States primarily because of poverty. People look for a better way of life for themselves and their family. The journey is dangerous and arduous—as the crossing of the Mediterranean that African immigrants endure. Because the border in populated areas is so heavily fortified by the United States, people are forced to cross the vast desert region that forms part of the border. Over the years, many have died in the treacherous crossing. I remember the story told by a woman some years ago about enduring a long ride in the back of a container piled high with immigrants. She could barely breathe. Praying,

---

3. http://vq.vassar.edu/issues/2012/02/vassar-today/at-the-border-nation-god-and-human-rights.html

The Preaching Mexican Immigrant Community in the United States

sure she would die, suddenly the back of the trailer opened, and the people were allowed to emerge, immediately running for fear of the authorities. The "luxury" of the container truck is now gone, yielding to the more dangerous foot crossing. Just in the Arizona border region in 2012, one hundred fifty seven corpses of Mexican migrants were found.[4] Once people are "settled," they fare no better. Undocumented immigrants have no medical benefits and live under constant threat of deportation. Unscrupulous employers threaten to turn them in to immigration authorities if they complain of low salaries and poor working conditions. Deportation is one worry among many. Lacking medical insurance, migrants are vulnerable to health problems readily treatable in other circumstances. Medical treatment for serious conditions is often not sought for lack of insurance or funds.

There is also danger in the workplace. I have already mentioned that some years ago in one of the communities I pastored, a young man working in an oyster factory was pinned by a forklift against a wall in a large commercial refrigerator. No one could hear his cries for help, and he died of hypothermia. In another case, Mexican and Salvadoran workers were not told of a chemical hazard where they were working in "environmental cleanup." Neither were they properly trained in HAZMAT nor given the proper equipment and clothing required for protection. Some began to complain of sores on their feet and hands that would not heal; eventually, one died.

When the Church community of the Holy Spirit in Kent, WA, met for prayer that December evening, the *Posada*, a traditional Mexican prayer used during the days leading to Christmas, was celebrated. In the *Posada*, Mary and Joseph go from station to station, singing "in the name of heaven" and asking for *"posada"*—room in the inn. Will the answer be "yes" or "no"? The poor preaching Church invited the dominant community to reflect that evening: will we say "yes," will we open our eyes to daily deportations, will we be concerned about the abuse of the migrant

---

4. http://www.huffingtonpost.com/leanne-torymurphy/dying-to-cross-migrants-c_b_4521221.html.

Part Three: Among

in the United States? The *posada* was a powerful prayer—a Holy Preaching—that called people, Mexican and Anglo, to action for justice. Preaching is more than words. It is the Word existing as community, the Spirit among the people in the voice of the poor, praxis for justice.

. . .

For Advent 2011, I chose what I thought was an innocent theme for preaching through the season. That particular year was commemorated as the five-hundredth anniversary of perhaps the most important sermon for social justice ever preached. The small Dominican community on the island of Quisquella, called by the Spanish *conquistadores* "La Española" (present-day Haiti and the Dominican Republic), preached this cry for justice. I have already referred to this pivotal event in the history of preaching.

In September 1510, a group of four Dominican friars arrived on Quisquella to minister to the Spanish colonists. The Dominicans were horrified at the conditions in which they found the indigenous *Taíno* population—abused, maltreated, and murdered by the colonists—mostly in the gold mines under Spanish control. The Dominicans decided to study and pray, analyzing the reality, for almost a year. At the end of the process, they pursued the path Dominicans are known for—the Holy Preaching. The decision was taken as a community, and their best preacher was selected—Antonio de Montesinos. After inviting all the prominent leaders with the pretext of a holiday celebration, Montesinos strongly denounced the bewildered colonists for their grave injustices. The colonists were furious and demanded a retraction. On the following Sunday, though, Montesinos preached again, telling the colonists this time that the Dominicans had decided as a community that sacramental absolution would be withheld from every colonist who did not give freedom to the *Taíno* slaves.[5]

---

5. For a more in-depth look, see Lorenz, *Montesinos' Legacy*, a collection of essays from a symposium on the occasion of the 500th anniversary of the Montesinos preaching.

The Preaching Mexican Immigrant Community in the United States

Five hundred years later as Advent 2011 unfolded, I treated a different aspect of the Montesinos preaching every Sunday, tying the major themes to Mexican immigrant reality in the United States. I sincerely believed the preaching would be well-received because it dealt with an historical reality; in addition, the Dominicans were asking Catholic parish communities throughout the world to reflect on this important patrimony of the Holy Preaching. It was history, I thought, and hopefully interesting. But I was in for a surprise! The Mexican immigrant community received the preaching well and was touched by this little known story, finding it helpful in understanding the injustices they were suffering. But a number in the English-speaking community were . . . not so happy! Antonio de Montesinos, Pedro de Córdoba, and Bartolomé de Las Casas—the names most often associated with this community of Dominican friars committed to justice for the *Taíno*—are not commonly known, even among specialists in historical theology. But they were greeted with joy in the migrant community. These friars who caused so much "trouble" for the sixteenth century colonists still caused controversy in the twenty-first century. They are proud heritage of the poor preaching Church for all ages. What do these courageous friars fearlessly preaching justice for the oppressed have to say to the Mexican immigrant community? What do they say to the dominant community about opening the doors of the southern border, about immigration reform? What do they say to the poor preaching Church?

Much has been written about the life, theology, and ministry of Dietrich Bonhoeffer. He has made an indispensable contribution to contemporary Christian theology, most notably in ecclesiology. It is often said that Bonhoeffer's theology is especially pertinent to present reality—to *context*. What would happen if immigration, lack of legal documentation, deportation, and other questions touching the Mexican community in the United States were seen in the light of Bonhoeffer's ecclesiology? Does a theology formulated in the context of Nazi Germany have anything to say to Mexican immigrants in the United States today? These questions may be rightly asked of the first Dominican friars in the New

Part Three: Among

World as well. What do they offer, contextually, to the Mexican immigrant community in the United States?

In the case of the Advent 2011 preaching, the Mexican migrant community strongly identified with the contextual situation of the Dominican friars in solidarity with the indigenous *Taíno* through the Holy Preaching. I received many comments from people wanting to know more about the friars, wanting to imitate their example of courage, grateful that they had preached on behalf of the indigenous and oppressed poor. But there was a deeper question. Many wondered how *they*—the *pueblo*—could preach on behalf of justice. Can the immigrant community itself become the Holy Preaching, a sacrament of Christ among the poor? The question animated the six parish *comunidades eclesiales de base*, "base ecclesial communities," small gatherings of people who come together weekly to pray the Sunday scriptures and apply them to the immigrant context they live. The communities are named for the early Christian communities: Ephesus, Antioch, Galatia, Damascus, Jerusalem, and Philippi. Over the years, they have studied, prayed, and reflected on the questions they ask: why are Mexican immigrants, largely undocumented and among the poorest of the poor in the United States—why are we *here*, *now*, at this *time*? How are we to proclaim the good news to the dominant community? The *pueblo* is aware that the immediate reason is the search for a better life. Often they take jobs no one else will accept. They are paid the lowest wages, barely earning enough to feed their families and pay rent and utilities; and yet much of their paycheck returns to support family in Mexico. But people in the CEBs (*comunidades eclesiales de base*) ask: is there *another* reason we are here? Are we called and sent, animated by the Spirit of Life, to proclaim the gospel to others in our situation—but also to the dominant community in the United States? Are we, as José Comblin says, the *voice* of the Spirit?

Mexican immigrants are inspired by the stories of Bartolomé de Las Casas, Pedro de Córdoba, Antonio de Montesinos, and the cry for justice from the Holy Preaching in December 1511. They have likewise been inspired by others, including Dietrich

The Preaching Mexican Immigrant Community in the United States

Bonhoeffer. What does a German pastor-theologian martyred by the Nazis over seventy years ago have to say to the Mexican immigrant community in the United States? The base communities gather as one on a monthly basis for an evening of study and reflection. Often the questions Bonhoeffer dealt with in Nazi Germany, or those posed by the Montesinos preaching, are studied: solidarity with the victim, freedom, the Church as "Christ existing as community," the Church as Person, how to live in the midst of persecution, oppression, and injustice, martyrdom as testimony. They know that the early Church under the Roman Empire faced similar questions. In short, how do we become the poor preaching Church, the *Sacra Praedicatio*?

The Mexican immigrant Church asks radical questions and invites the Church in the United States to deeper reflection. Will we listen to the good news proclaimed by the poor preaching Church and the testimony given by them? The dominant Church must decide: are we members of the Empire or the community that follows the poor Jesus Christ and listens to the voice of the Spirit in the poor *pueblo*?

Chapter 12

The Poor Church as Preacher

Traditionally, there are four marks of the Church professed from earliest times—one, holy, catholic, and apostolic. They characterize the very being of the Church. Without them, the Church cannot be *community*—the people of God, the body of Christ, and the creation of the Holy Spirit. The marks are essential aspects of the ecclesial community that bespeak who we are: One, like the Holy Trinity in unity but diverse in expression, culture, language, custom, and unique ways of being local community, diverse and undivided, nevertheless one; holy, though sinful, God's holy people "in-dwelled" by the Holy Spirit, whose body is the Holy Body; catholic, local communities forming a world-wide, universal Church; and apostolic, founded upon the apostles by the inspiration of the Holy Spirit who, in our own historical context, animates Church community just as the first New Testament communities.

Might there be other marks? Could other words today express the fullness of these four traditional marks? Edward Schillebeeckx refers to "solidarity with the poor" as an "essential mark of the Church." Latin American theologians agree—one cannot speak of Church without the poor. Pope Francis solidly associates the poor with the Church community: "How I would like a poor

The Poor Church as Preacher

Church of the poor." I have already spoken of *loci theologici*. Can we speak of solidarity with the poor as a fifth mark of the Church, suggested in recent years by the theology of liberation, indigenous theology, ecofeminist theology, the base communities, and other theologies of the poor? Is this fifth mark essential to the believing Christian and his or her orthodoxy (and orthopraxis)? If essential, as Schillebeeckx says, what does this mean for the theology of preaching? Is the Church obliged to be faithful to the fifth mark not only through solidarity with the poor but by *listening* to the poor preaching Church? Is this mark of solidarity with the poor best expressed by the poor Church's solidarity in *preaching* and the wealthy Church's solidarity in *listening*?

It must be said that a "fifth mark" of the universal Church is nothing new. It has been present with us since earliest times, beginning with the New Testament period, through post-apostolic times, the Fathers and Mothers, medieval times, the Barmen Declaration, to our contemporary context, expressed especially in the documents of the Second Vatican Council, *Medellín* and *Puebla*, ecclesial documents on economic justice and immigration rights, and, most recently, by Pope Francis in *Evangelii Gaudium* and *Laudato Si*. Solidarity with the poor has always "marked" us as a believing community.

Theologians refer to a new paradigm for theology today.[1] Perhaps the same should be said for preaching. The context of preaching has changed, along with the world. But there has been little consequence for the way we write books about preaching, teach homiletics, or actually *do* preaching from Sunday to Sunday. The pastor still is the usual Sunday preacher. Homily preparation is often a struggle and not a joy. And then there are the constant parish commitments that consume the pastor's time—meetings, visits, staff supervision, and administration. Often Saturday morning comes around, and the pastor finds that he or she has put little time into the Sunday preaching. Not important, he tells himself. He is about the business of the Lord, so the Lord—and the people—will forgive if there has simply not been the time for proper

---

1. See Küng, *Great Christian Thinkers*, and Boff, *Ecología*.

preparation. I am reminded of a cartoon I saw many years ago in the Catholic periodical *Critic* (now no longer published). The pastor is casually draped over the pulpit and announces, "I didn't have the time to prepare my homily this weekend, so why doesn't someone just throw out a topic, and I'll wing it" (!). The humor is well-taken, and the cartoon pokes fun at what is often the perennial attitude of many Catholic pastors toward the Sunday homily—it is a "necessary evil" that goes along with ordained ministry, more often than not the last in a long list of priorities.

Am I painting the picture too negatively? Perhaps. I know that many pastors put great effort into the Holy Preaching. They begin their week reflecting on the Scriptures for the following Sunday; they pray over the Scriptures with parishioners; they take the necessary time for studying the texts that will be preached; and much care is put into the crafting of the final product. But for others, Saturday is greeted with empty hands and the rush to the nearest homiletic service. Is it a wonder that one of the major complaints from parishioners is the quality of the Sunday preaching?

This sad state of affairs is not particularly the preacher's fault but the result of centuries of neglect of the *Holy Preaching*. The Second Vatican Council has tried to recover the importance of the word in Catholic liturgy, and, most recently, Pope Francis' excellent apostolic exhortation *Evangelii Gaudium* devoted an entire section to the importance of preaching. He writes from the perspective of a doctor who knows well the physical health of his or her patient. Catholic theology and pastoral practice have given short shrift to the ministry of the word. Although preaching is a charism of the baptized, the Catholic Church (and it is not alone in this) has restricted the "liturgical homily" on Sundays to the ordained presbyter or deacon. "Lay" people—especially women!—need not apply. The "five to seven minute rule," the obligatory story-telling too often focused on the pastor, the "dumbing down" of preaching, and other "enlightened" approaches have attempted to modernize the Catholic pulpit. But I do not think this is what Vatican II, or *Evangelii Gaudium*, has in mind.

The Poor Church as Preacher

I can't help but wonder about the "state of preaching"—are we not only missing the boat but not yet even on the dock? It is high time, I believe, for a new paradigm of preaching—a preaching that does not make the Sunday homily an unpleasant task for preacher and congregation but directs itself to the *Holy Preaching*, concerning and springing forth from women and men, young people and children, our wounded world, a preaching that is gift of the poor to the Church community and the world. How might such preaching look?

Leonardo Boff, in speaking of the new paradigm for theology, says that it must be "mutual, communal, and reciprocal."[2] Can these three adjectives be used to describe how the poor preaching Church can go about its task? Where do we find mutuality, communality, and reciprocity?

St. Dominic, as already noted, first applied the word "preaching" (*praedicatio*) not so much to the formal act of liturgical preaching as to an entire community of people. His first communities of Dominicans, both women and men, were called the *Sacra Praedicatio*—the "Holy Preaching." Preaching, if it is to be anything, must be integrally connected to a people, a *community*. Can we recuperate this ancient view of preaching and apply it to the new preaching paradigm? I remind the reader of Fr. Gonzalo Ituarte, the Dominican friar who talks about how the Sunday preaching is done among the base indigenous communities in Chiapas. The people form a circle in the church, including the one presiding at the Eucharist or coordinating the service of word and communion. After the proclamation of the readings, everyone participates in the Holy Preaching as a *community*. All opinions are valued, from the *padrecito* to the youngest child. The preaching is radically communal, coming from the Church, for the Church, within the Church, and to the Church—a "synergy" of the Spirit of Life and the people beloved of God. All are given the opportunity to speak. When the preaching is finished, the celebration of the Eucharist continues. The community is *mutual* and *reciprocal*.

2. Boff, *Ecologia*, 128–43.

Part Three: Among

The traditional notion of preaching is generally based on what one of my seminary professors called "the mug and the jug" methodology (James Dunning). In this pedagogical model, there is an empty, large jug, whose only purpose is to be filled with water from a "mug." The mug (the teacher) faithfully goes to the faucet of books, previous lectures, libraries, and talks for a daily "fill up" with water, which, in turn, is faithfully poured into the "jug" (the student). Over the course of the student's formal education, he or she is eventually "filled" with all kinds of ideas, but without much deeper reflection. The methodology hopes that personal integration will happen as the student matures. But for the time being, the student *needs* this constant fill-up. He or she is finally so "full" that there is room for nothing else, no original idea. The role of the student in this pedagogy is to receive passively (and without question) what the teacher wants to impart in knowledge. Likewise preaching, in this mug and jug model, is seen as the "imparting" of the "eternal truths of the tradition" (the gospel?) to the "students," the community of believers turned passive listeners who come, week after week, for their "fill up" of religion. This has also been called the "gas station" model! Unfortunately, even the most enlightened congregations become passive "hearers of the word" (*never* Rahner's intention in his great work with the same name), while the preacher is the one "in the know" who generously shares of *his* (male in the Catholic world) font of knowledge. There is no reciprocity between teacher and student in the mug and jug, because reciprocity assumes dialogue. Neither is there mutuality or communality.

If this is the case in well-to-do communities, what of the poor? Historically, we get an idea from the colonial churches. The work of the traditional missioner, whether Catholic or Protestant, has generally been done from this pedagogy. The mug was gold-plated and privileged beyond imagination, while the jug was inferior, poor, and uneducated. Colonial conquests, as the case in Latin America, were veritable genocides where cross and sword were undistinguishable. The indigenous populations, with very few exceptions (Pedro de Córdoba, Antonio de Montesinos, and

The Poor Church as Preacher

Bartolomé de Las Casas), were colonially subjected economically, racially, sexually, biologically, *and* religiously. The missioners came as the enlightened colonizers who would bring "civilization" to the "savages." They had the only true faith. The indigenous were "idolaters" who needed only conversion at risk of the "fires of hell." This mission superiority continued throughout the mid-twentieth century and beyond in many Christian sectors.

With the Second Vatican Council and equivalent reforms in Orthodox and mainline Protestant communities, things began to change. Congregations like Maryknoll, Scarborough, Mill Hill, the Columbans, as well as traditional orders such as the Dominicans, the Jesuits, and the Franciscans, began to take the missiology of the Council and apply it directly and pastorally to mission. Third-World bishops conferences such as CELAM (the Latin American bishops) were even more radical in their approach. Especially in the two conferences immediately following the Second Vatican Council, *Medellín* (1968) and *Puebla* (1979), the bishops incarnated the faith in the context of the poor. The results were startling. As with any revolution, reactionary forces were not far behind, and the "mug and jug" preaching methodology is what still predominates—with especially tragic consequences in poor communities.

Comunidades Eclesiales de Base—Base Ecclesial Communities—are on the forefront of the search for a new pastoral-theological pedagogy, not only in catechetical formation but in the approach to the Holy Preaching. Brazilian theologian Alvaro Barreiro, SJ, says that the people of the base communities are moving "from hearers to preachers of the gospel":

> In the midst of that vast throng of poor people among whom the CEBs (base ecclesial communities) have been established there is being created through the force of the Spirit, a Church in which the poor are, simultaneously, the evangelized and evangelizers, the privileged recipients and the conveyors of the good news of the Kingdom of God. Among the far-flung messianic people, the CEBs are one of the places where one can breathe more deeply and purely the air of hope in the justice and mercy of the Kingdom of God which is absolutely vital to the

Church.... Instilled with this "hope against all hope," the CEBs are trying to live, in a demanding way and under the extremely difficult conditions of their environment, the good news which they have accepted, celebrating it jubilantly in worship and proclaiming it courageously to those who have not yet heard it.[3]

The poor preach in many ways—through word, example, action, praxis, and life. In a parish I pastored for many years, the base ecclesial communities proclaim the good news to the poor: sacramental preparation programs, baptism formation for the parish community, the *Catequesis Familiar* (Family Catechesis) program of first communion preparation placing special emphasis on meetings with parents, feeding programs for the Anglo homeless, and, most especially, witness to the dominant Anglo community. Barreiro continues:

> The poor of the CEBs are not only proclaiming the good news of liberation to other poor people who have not yet heard it and, in a different manner, to those who are the direct cause of their oppression. They are also, and primarily, evangelizing the Church, from which they received the gospel, through witness to the force of their faith, the courage of their hope, the efficacy of their love, and the living experience of fraternity. The CEBs are for the Church . . . primarily a constant, pressing appeal to conversion.[4]

Brazilian Jesuit Marcelo Acevedo stresses that the base communities comprise a "new way" of being Church.[5] This "new way" is founded in the recent ecclesial and sacramental paradigms coming out of the Second Vatican Council, Latin American episcopal conferences, and the pastoral experience of the poor in Latin America. In this new paradigm, the Church is primary sacrament (Karl Rahner, Edward Schillebeeckx), the *sacramentum mundi*, enabling the world to see its own sacramentality. The Church

---

3. Barreiro, *Basic Ecclesial Communities*, 64.
4. Ibid., 67.
5. Acevedo, *Basic Ecclesial Communities in Brazil*.

The Poor Church as Preacher

community is "possessed" by the Holy Spirit, who gives it its mission. It is often said that the Church "has" a mission. But in the words of Alan Figueroa Deck, SJ, the *mission* has the Church! In the new paradigm the Church, in its very being, is *missionary*. The poor are seen as the primary missioners, evangelizers, and *preachers*. The base communities proclaim the gospel to the Church and to the world. They are now no longer the "evangelized"; rather, they are the evangelizers.[6] The dominant community, the wealthy Church of the First World, must place itself in solidarity with the poor by letting themselves be *converted* by the poor, to the poor. Thus the poor Church is the preaching Church:

> The evangelizing Church must begin by *undergoing conversion* itself. It does this by opting, as did Jesus Christ, to favor the poor as the ones to whom the proclamation of the Good News is addressed ... This change of social locations, combined with an awareness and understanding of the Church's mission, should have enormous consequences. It should prompt the Church to assume their struggles and sufferings, to assimilate their culture, to identify with them, and to read reality from their perspective. Thus, the gospel is announced to the poor to make it possible for them to liberate themselves; and they are the starting point because they are the *bearers of the proclaimed message* (italics mine). The Church now begins to prize the poor as *evangelizers* as well. The gospel is announced by them, even to the Church itself, by virtue of the perception given to them by the Spirit. It is a perception of the word of God ... The gospel message is proclaimed from the angle of the poor to those in the Church who are not poor, and by this Church to the world of the rich as well. This proclamation aims at their liberation also.[7]

This poor preaching Church is a *pueblo* that gives priority to *praxis*. For a number of years, theology has turned to practical ethics to understand its task as a reflection on Christian praxis.

---

6. Boff, *New Evangelization*.
7. Acevedo, *Basic Ecclesial Communities*, 191.

Part Three: Among

Ethics is turning toward what Emmanuel Levinas calls "the face of the other." The other is person.[8] The other as person seeks mutuality and reciprocity in community. Juan Carlos Scannone, SJ, an Argentinian theologian and mentor of Pope Francis, builds on Levinas by saying that the contemporary challenge in theology is the turn from metaphysics—"being"—to the ethical invitation represented by the face of the other.[9] This post-modern turn to the other—the "turning away" from the Cartesian subject—is best expressed by the priority of ethics and praxis. Dietrich Bonhoeffer felt that ethics trumped most every theological endeavor, considering *Ethics* (*DBWE* 6), written in snippets during his last years, his monumental work. Good and evil, he said, could no longer be the subject solely of metaphysical ethics. Rather, he says, the will of God is primary. What is God's plan for creation, for humankind? Where is the face of the other? The victim took on a special significance for Bonhoeffer. Ethical questions are never merely theoretical, metaphysical. They always shed infinite light on the face of the person of the other, so that we instinctively know what to do in the given situation. This post-modern concern for the ethical leads directly to praxis, to which Latin American theology ascribes a central place:

> Latin American theologians take with utmost seriousness the situation in which they live . . . The one viewing this theology from a distance must never lose sight of the intimate relationship between this theology and the context in which it has emerged. . . . To actually understand liberation theology apart from its historical context is simply not possible. The word that is most frequently used to describe this persistent orientation of liberation theology to its socioeconomic and historical context is the word *praxis*. Praxis is chosen by the theologians of liberation to express that which is distinctive about their thought. The word praxis incorporates the entire scope of liberation theology as it moves from an encounter with the Latin American context of poverty and oppression

---

8. Panikkar, *Christophany*, 64–65.
9. Scannone, *Religión y Nuevo Pensamiento*, 56–58.

The Poor Church as Preacher

into socioeconomic analysis and theological reflection and then returns to the task of constructing a more just future for Latin America. Praxis-orientation thus refers to a way of theologizing that never loses sight of its own participation in the liberation process.[10]

Christian *action*, praxis, is central to the Holy Preaching. Latin American theologians utilize the words "praxis" and "orthopraxis" (as contrasted with traditional orthodoxy) to describe what is central to the theological task. Gustavo Gutiérrez calls theology a "critical reflection on praxis," but theology—and preaching—is also praxis. If theology is primarily ecclesiology, it must be praxis centered in the *community* of the poor preaching Church—the Holy Preaching. The new paradigm for the Holy Preaching must be, in Boff's words, *mutual, communal,* and *reciprocal.* Jesus proclaims the good news by announcing the year of favor:

> The Spirit of the Lord is upon me, because he has anointed me to bring good news to the poor. He has sent me to proclaim release to the captives and recovery of sight to the blind, to let the oppressed go free, to proclaim the year of the Lord's favor." And he rolled up the scroll, gave it back to the attendant, and sat down. The eyes of all in the synagogue were fixed on him. Then he began to say to them, "Today this scripture has been fulfilled in your hearing" (Luke 4:18–21).

The Holy Preaching is the presence of Christ announcing the good news to the poor today. May all of us have ears to hear!

---

10. Nessan, *Orthopraxis or Heresy*, 18–19.

Chapter 13

The Church and the Holy Trinity

When we hear the word "Trinity," we immediately think unfathomable mystery. Though central to our faith, we have trouble relating to the God "Three in One." We believe God is Trinity who has overcome loneliness and isolation, communion among Father, Son, and Holy Spirit, a beautiful and perfect sharing to imitate in our relationships. This imitation, though, is difficult. It seems far from us—our humanity, our concerns, our limitations. In the final analysis, a sharing among Persons "spiritual" and "perfect" appears infinitely distant. It is, after all, a *divine* communion, isn't it?

Thus through centuries of theological parsing ever more removed from human experience, the Divine Three, our central belief, has, unfortunately, grown hazy and dogmatized into a closed, masculine, and arcane theoretical system. What is needed is fresh thinking that respects the tradition but also speaks to our context—thinking rooted in our experience of humanity and creation. I invite you to dare to think in new ways about the Holy Trinity, above all because at this decisive moment of our history, full of difficult questions and institutional crises, the very survival of life is at stake, says Brazilian theologian Ivone Gebara.[1] She does not overstate the case: we *must* radically rework the "contemplation

---

1. Gebara, "The Trinity," 13.

The Church and the Holy Trinity

of the Holy Trinity." It is important because it is *the* theological task. The challenge for a "new paradigm" of Trinity is fidelity to traditional language but openness to varied ways of expressing reality for new and different contexts. This is of the utmost importance to the Holy Preaching. But how do we contemplate the Great Mystery? Three Divine Persons, One God? If the purpose of contemplation is *reality*, how does the "real" hold the content of divine community?

If we are to contemplate rightly the Holy Trinity in the twenty-first century, we must do so with *real* eyes, *real* ears, and *real* hearts turned toward the poor. The Church community is the icon of the Holy Trinity, says Bruno Forte. It is there, then, where the Holy Trinity is contemplated. This contemplation occurs most especially in the preaching Church of the poor, in the *pueblo*.

The Church is universal and local at the same time. One does not take precedence over the other. They cannot be divided, like the Persons of the Holy Trinity; like the Divine Three, they are one Church in a rich expression of diversity within the local Churches. In the Trinity, there is difference but not division, diversity but not separation. This holds for the universal Church and its local manifestations. The Holy Trinity is infinitely present within the poorest, most forgotten, most oppressed local ecclesial communities. *This* specific local community of the poor—the poor preaching Church—is the presence, the icon, of the Holy Trinity to the fullest. Precisely for this reason, the local Church is the *full* expression of the universal Church. Fr. José Marins, theologian and mentor for the *comunidades eclesiales de base*, says that the local manifestation of the universal Church is the base community. One of the primary teachings of the Second Vatican Council, he says, is that the local Church *is* the presence of the universal Church in the fullest sense, its manifestation at the local level:

> For us, the basic church community is the church itself, the universal sacrament of salvation, as it

Part Three: Among

continues the mission of Christ—Prophet, Priest, and Pastor. This is what makes it a community of faith, worship, and love. Its mission is explicitly expressed on all levels—the universal, the diocesan, and the local, or basic.[2]

This local Church, the *comunidad eclesial de base*, is privileged expression of the universal Church precisely because it is poor. Those in solidarity with the poor throughout the world join them in the universal Church through their own local ecclesial manifestations. The poor of the local Churches—and the poor of the world—are the "privileged ones" of the Triune God:

> Jesus confirms this privilege of the poor, since He proclaims that they are to inherit the Kingdom. God, who undertakes to correct human mistakes, will give the keys of the Kingdom to the poor, for in the Kingdom justice will reign. It is natural that the victims of injustice and exploitation should be the first to receive the privilege of the Kingdom. Moreover, in Jesus we find a model of the way of life of the poor man who is also a "servant of Yahweh"; he is not resigned to his poverty, but practices the hope which kindles hope in others too.[3]

If the Church community is the icon of the Holy Trinity, then the base ecclesial community— the preaching Church of the poor—becomes, in the deepest sense, the *privileged icon* of the Holy Trinity. Here we "do theology" like the Fathers and Mothers: we contemplate the Holy Trinity through the contemplation of its icon. With these introductory remarks, let us now briefly revisit traditional Trinitarian theology and belief.

. . .

The classic expression of Christian faith in the Holy Trinity is: "Three Divine Persons, One God." These Persons are undivided,

---

2. Marins, "Comunidades Eclesiaes de Base na América Latina," 27, quoted from Boff, *Ecclesiogenesis*, 12.

3. De Santa Ana, *Good News to the Poor*, 95.

The Church and the Holy Trinity

inseparable in their unity. But they are different from one another, diverse; they are unique. The challenge for the Christian community in speaking about the Holy Trinity has been to avoid two extremes: turning the Trinity of Persons into three gods; or disregarding the diversity among the Persons so that, in effect, the Three Persons are merged into one, that is, the Three Persons become one "personality" instead of one God. The first extreme has been called "tritheism" and the second "modalism." These epithets have, at times, been unjustly hurled at sincere theologians in the struggle to articulate the Holy Mystery Who is the Trinity. Even today, the Eastern Orthodox Church has been called "tritheist" by the some Catholics; and the Catholic Church has been called "modalist" by the some Orthodox. As an interesting aside, the two great Karls of twentieth century theology, Barth and Rahner, have both been accused of modalism! In the attempt to properly speak about the Holy Trinity, we forget that the Triune God is, above all, *Holy Mystery* to be contemplated, not analyzed. This contemplation can begin in either the oneness of the Holy Mystery or the three-ness and still remain dogmatically orthodox.

However, when the icon contemplated is the poor preaching Church, the starting point must be *both* the oneness and the three-ness at the same time. Trinitarian theology has much to learn from the poor! The *pueblo* is one but diverse in its unity. Like the Trinity, oneness and three-ness are integral qualities of the preaching Church of the poor. Seen from Aquinas' *via negativa*, neither the Holy Trinity nor the Church community is "One" or "Three" in the popular, i.e., numeric sense. As has often been pointed out, the Triune God is not mathematics. We are not talking, as Boff says, of "one plus one plus one equals three." Rather, it is more "one plus one plus one equals One." The traditional marks of the Church remind us: one and holy (One God and one community), catholic and apostolic (local and diverse sent as leaven into the world by the Divine Three). The Church cannot be divided; the Trinity cannot be divided. The Church is one yet diverse; the Trinity is one yet diverse. The one Church is a community of diverse persons; the Trinity is community of diverse persons. The Church is relationship among persons; the Trinity is relationship among Persons.

The One Holy Trinity is Three Persons. The First Divine Person is "Father." *Abba* was the way Jesus addressed the Father. As Jeremias reminds us, it means "papa," "beloved father." So much more than biological, it is *relational*. As relational, it goes far beyond gender and expresses also the meaning of *imma*—"mama, beloved mother." The relationship between Father and the Son is where the New Testament Church began its reflection on the Holy Trinity. The Holy Spirit seals the relationship; but much more, the Spirit is *Person* in *relationship* with the Father and Son. The traditional word that best expresses the relationship among the Three is *perichoeresis*, virtually untranslatable but meaning "interpenetration," a relationship profound and mysterious in which the Three Persons "cross over" into one another without losing their uniqueness. *Perichoeresis* is manifested in both the oneness and three-ness. This crossing over into one another is the deepest intercommunication imaginable, making the Trinity One and Three at the same time. To use the language of contemporary psychology, the relation is life-giving, sustaining, utterly respectful of the other, wholly non-abusive.

The gospels speak primarily of the relationship between the Father and the Son, but what of the Holy Spirit? Of course, the Spirit is much referenced in the New Testament. But the Old Testament can be called the "book of the Spirit" *par excellence*. While the writers of the Hebrew Scriptures certainly did not think of the Spirit-*Ruah*-breath-wind of God as the Christian Third Person of the Holy Trinity, the First Testament is full of Spirit-*Ruah*. The creating Spirit (*Veni Creator Spiritus* is an ancient chant reminding us that the Spirit and creation are deeply intertwined) hovers over the *tohuwabohu*, the chaos (Gen 1:2), and out of chaos comes creative harmony. The darkness is not destroyed, it is "hovered" over; and God says, "Let there be light" (Gen 1:3). Whatever the "Big Bang" is ultimately—for that, too, is mystery—it creates *light*. The massive explosion becomes a gigantic flash, giving life to everything. The Spirit hovers over the nothingness (*creatio ex nihilo*) and

The Church and the Holy Trinity

brings about light, so that all else follows in the brightness of the light, the perichoeretic explosion, the "crossing over" giving life to everything in the life-giving Spirit. The Spirit continues creating life through the prophecy of Eldad and Medad (Num 11:25-29) and the judges (Judg 3:10, 6:34, 11:29, 13:24, 14:6, 19, 15:14). The Spirit "rushes" on Saul (1 Sam 10:6 ff, 11:6) and "departs" from him (1 Sam 16:14). King David is full of Spirit (1 Sam 16:13). Job knows "the Spirit of God has made me, and the breath of the Almighty gives me life" (Job 33:4). Azariah (2 Chr 15:1) and Jahziel (2 Chr 20:14) prophesy under the inspiration of the Spirit-*Ruah*. The prophet Joel says "your sons and your daughters shall prophesy, your old men shall dream dreams, your young men shall see visions," and even the servants, women and men, will have *Ruah* poured out upon them (Joel 2:28-29). The three books of Isaiah are full of Spirit (Isa 11:2, 30:1, 32:15, 34:16, 40:13, 44:3, 48:16, 59:21, 61:1, 63:10, 11, 14) as is the book of Ezekiel (Ezek 2:2, 3:12, 14, 24, 8:3, 11:1, 5, 24, 43:5), where the Spirit is promised to the people in covenant (Ezek 36:26-27, 39:29). The Suffering Servant of God (Isa 42:1) receives the Spirit to "bring forth justice to the nations." The prophet Micah speaks for the Spirit of the justice of God (Mic 3:8). God, says the prophet Zechariah to Zerubbabel, works "not by power or might" but by the Spirit *Ruah* (Zech 4:6). Most especially, the people of God seek the Spirit of life in prayer (Pss 51:11, 104:30, 139:7, 143:10).

In the New Testament, the work of the Holy Spirit in Jesus' ministry weighs heavily in the Synoptics, especially Luke (1:15, 35, 41, 67, 2:25-27, 3:16, 22, 4:1, 14, 18, 10:21, 11:13, 12:10, 12). If seen as a unit, Luke and Acts tell the story of Jesus, full of the Spirit, and his community of followers, inspired by the same Spirit. The gospel of John contains many references to the work of the Holy Spirit (John 1:31, 3:5, 8, 34, 4:23, 6:63, 7:39, 14:17, 26, 15:26, 16:13, 20:22). Perhaps the Acts of the Apostles, the story of the first Spirit-filled Church communities, was a primary reference for

Part Three: Among

St. Thomas Aquinas, who calls the Holy Spirit the "soul," the life-giving principle, of the Church community. The Holy Spirit brings about the "birth" of the Church community (Acts 2:1–13) and is so important in the creation of the community that there are over seventy references to the work of the Spirit in Acts.[4]

The Church community images the Holy Trinity in perichoeretic relationships. The relationship among Persons of the Holy Trinity is a model for the relationships among the members of the body of Christ and the creation of the Holy Spirit. The Persons of Jesus and the Spirit are, in St. Irenaeus' Trinitarian theology, the two hands of God. These hands send, or perhaps better said, "push" the Church community, into mission—which, in the words of Fr. Alan Deck, *possesses* the Church. He simply says, "The *mission* has a Church."[5]

In the New Testament, perhaps the most explicit reference to the Trinity—and it is directly connected to baptism and the mission of the people of God—is Matt 28:19 ("Go therefore and make disciples of all nations, baptizing them in the name of the Father and of the Son and of the Holy Spirit"). It has been called the "Great Commission" of the Church. Through the waters of baptism, the Divine Three send us forth in mission. José Ignacio Gonzalez Faus, SJ, says that the gospel of Matthew, particularly as the risen Jesus sends the disciples forth in the name of the Trinity, is an entire "Trinitarian immersion."[6] The mission absorbs the poor preaching Church. It immerses it, possesses it, animates it, and inspires it. It is the great call to action, gospel praxis on behalf of justice. If hands are primarily used for work and action, the hands of God, Jesus and Spirit, "push" the poor preaching community into action for justice (remember St. Irenaeus' "two hands" image of the Trinity and José Comblin's "action of God"?).

Traditionally, this "pushing" is the work of the economic Trinity. Without discussing Rahner's brilliant *theologoumenon* that the economic and the immanent Trinity are one and the same, for

4. White, *The Holy Spirit*, 141.
5. Deck, Preacher's Conference, Bellevue, WA, 2006.
6. Gonzalez Faus, *Al Tercer Dia*, 43.

The Church and the Holy Trinity

practical purposes we *must* talk of the *oikonomia* (economy) of the Trinity. That is how we *know* the divine Trinitarian action. The *oikonomia* is the "household" of the Triune God, the place where Holy Trinity *acts*. The action of the Trinity in the economy is the Holy Preaching, living, breathing, animating through its icon the poor preaching Church in synergy with the Triune God, in whom "we live and move and have our being" (Acts 17:28). Preaching is the action of the Church community, the action of the two hands of God touching, caressing, encouraging, *and* pushing. This action is subversive. It "under-turns" the order (or disorder) of things. The word "subversion" is similar to "conversion." Conversion, biblical *metanoia*, is a "turning around" of the heart and mind.

I have sometimes preached that prayer is "subversive activity." Often we pray without reflecting. What if we were *really* conscious that God gives what we ask? We should be careful about what we pray for, because God *does* answer prayer—though not in the way we often expect! Like prayer, preaching, too, is often carelessly done. As Barbara Brown Taylor observes, most preachers these days enter the Sunday pulpit more easily than if they were getting into the car to go to the corner store for a carton of milk. Who wants to be a "conduit for lightening," she asks? Congregants often expect nothing significant from the Sunday preaching, because many preachers themselves expect nothing.[7]

Blessed Rupert Mayer, SJ, a priest who, like Dietrich Bonhoeffer, stood up to Adolf Hitler and the Nazis, said that he joined the Jesuits because they were a persecuted community and that they would prepare him well for the "struggle."[8] The struggle against the Nazis would be waged, for Mayer, in the crucible of the Holy Preaching. It is said that he was not particularly dynamic in his preaching. Rather, he preached on behalf of *justice* without fear of the consequences. People flocked to his preaching because they saw in Blessed Rupert a prophetic man who had something important to say. In fact, it was his preaching that got him into trouble. During his first court hearing with the Nazis, the evidence

---

7. Taylor, *When God Is Silent*, 86.
8. Migoya, *El Jesuita Que Se Enfrentó a Hitler*, 22.

Part Three: Among

they used against him was his *preaching*.⁹ In Munich (including preaching at the train station to workers), he preached an average of seventy homilies monthly. He died in November of 1945—while preaching.¹⁰

Preaching is the subversive activity of the Triune God, whose icon is the preaching Church of the poor. Preaching gives witness to the good news of Jesus through the action of proclamation. It is not an exercise in rhetoric, though good preaching will make use of rhetoric for the sake of the gospel.¹¹ It is not meant to "uplift the congregation," though good preaching has consolation of the poor as one of its goals. The primary purpose of preaching is the *proclamation of the gospel*. That got Jesus into trouble. How can it be otherwise for preachers today—as has been pointed out by Joaquin Antonio Peñalosa?¹² And yet we continue to teach homiletics whose purpose is persuasion, edification, and consolation. Often, this is even the sole basis for evaluation. That which is subversive is difficult to listen to. It challenges. It judges. It *disturbs*. In short . . . it invites people to reflect. A preaching community will do the same, for it is, at core, the action of the two hands of the Triune God in the poor community of the Holy Preaching. The poor preaching Church is the icon where the Holy Trinity—God Father-Mother, Jesus Son-Brother, Holy Spirit of life—is contemplated. Then, miracle of miracles! The Word is born anew through the sacred contemplation, and, *contemplata aliis tradere*, the fruits of contemplation are shared in the Holy Preaching.

---

9. Ibid., 96–103.

10. Kidder, "Bonhoeffer in the Company of Martyrs," https://www.youtube.com/watch?v=aQwYZ4qT50w

11. Resner, *Preacher and Cross*.

12. Peñalosa, *Manual*, 5–6.

Chapter 14

All Creation Groans
Preaching and the Community of Life

> For the creation waits with eager longing for the revealing of the children of God. We know that the whole creation has been groaning in labor pains until now; and not only the creation, but we ourselves, who have the first fruits of the Spirit, groan inwardly while we wait for adoption, the redemption of our bodies (Rom 8:19, 22–23).

Preaching *groans* more than speaks: the groans of the poor preaching Church, the groans of humanity—and also the groans of creation, the entire universe. The *perichoeresis* of the Holy Trinity is discerned through the groaning of the universe. It is present with Mother Earth as she groans with her children, the poor.

Maryknoll priest Fr. Thomas Burns, who has worked in Perú his entire ministry, speaks of the difficult time that the Peruvian people experienced in the 1980s, caught between *Sendero Luminoso* ("The Shining Path," a radical terrorist group) and the military and police forces. It was also a time when the *pueblo* suffered extreme economic distress. Fr. Burns felt helpless, not knowing what to say. What could he preach, he asked? A woman spoke up: *Danos una palabra de aliento, Padrecito*—"give us a word of hope."

Part Three: Among

In the midst of the groans of the preaching Church, the poor are hungry for a word of hope.

We live in a time of grave danger for the poor and Mother Earth. However, people *are* beginning to see the integral connection between the poor and creation and the damage being done to both. The oppression of the poor by gigantic impersonal networks of multinational companies deeply involves the oppression of Mother Earth. Theology, faith, the preaching Church, and the groaning poor simply can no longer be disconnected from concern for Mother Earth—*Pacha Mama*, as the Andean people call her.

Theologians are paying closer attention to ecological questions. This is especially true of two Brazilians, Ivone Gebara and Leonardo Boff, who have written that the question of ecology is inseparable from the poor. Both have been reflecting on poverty and the ecology since the 1990s and continue to publish around these themes. Boff has been especially prolific in the English and Spanish translations, but Gebara brings the perspective of many years of accompanying poor women in the Brazilian urban slums. Her theology is deeply insightful and has been referred to as "ecofeminism." She is one of its best-known voices. Ecofemisism, in the words of Anna Case-Winters, is a "broad and diverse movement" with a number of "shared presuppositions" such as: the "connection between the oppression of women and the oppression of nature," the "hierarchical dualism" leading to a "logic of domination . . . that must be dismantled for the sake of social justice and ecological responsibility" and replaced by a "transformative worldview" where "mutuality, equality, and solidarity" are the hallmarks.[1] Gebara has expressed indebtedness to North American ecofeminists like Rosemary Radford Ruether.[2] The unique view she represents is the perspective of a Third-World theologian concerned about feminist questions, theology, the poor, and creation. Hers is a new way of "doing theology":

---

1. Case-Winters, *Reconstructing a Christian Theology*, 63.

2. Ruether, *Christianity and Ecofeminism*, 97–110, for an excellent summary of ecofeminism and Ruether's indebtedness to Gebara, 105–108.

The expression "women doing theology" is new, as is the explication of what the expression means. Previously, there was never any mention of sexual difference with regard to those who wrote theology, since it was obvious that the task was something proper to men. Today it would seem that the matter is no longer obvious, and the gender of the authors must be specified. Gender is understood not only as a biological difference prior even to birth, but especially as a cultural dimension, that is, as a stance or an aspect that affects the production of other cultural values, of other kinds of human interrelationship and other ways of thinking.³

This new way of doing theology is especially evident in women. Gebara says that women bring the "elements of everyday life" into the way in which they speak about God.⁴ They are more open to diversity, complexity, difference, and plurality; these bring a fresh perspective ot the theological endeavor.⁵ Most especially, Gebara says, women have taken pro-active roles in the base ecclesial communities. They bring special gifts to the communities because they offer a different approach to traditional male-dominated ministry. Women represent a "new way of organizing ministry."⁶

Gebara, a Canoness of St. Augustine, integrates concern for personalism with the deeply communitarian sense of Latin American reality and an Eastern Christian approach to theological questions (she is of Lebanese heritage). She also appreciates the urgency of ecological questions. "Ivone Gebara," say Anne Marie Dalton and Henry Simmons, "speaks of the individual human body as a Cosmic Body because of the intimate connections of humans to the entire universe. She also calls our 'larger self' the Sacred Body of the Cosmos."⁷ Gebara strongly challenges male-dominated Western theology to move from the metaphysical preoccupation it has traditionally enshrined to an epistemological theology free

3. Tamez, *Through Her Eyes*, 37.
4. Ibid., 41.
5. Ibid., 46.
6. Ibid., 47–48.
7. Dalton, *Ecology and the Practice of Hope*, 80.

Part Three: Among

of metaphysical dualism.⁸ This rejection of dualism, along with its consequent "anthropocentrism," is typical of ecofeminist theology.⁹ Rosemary Radford Ruether summarizes Gebara's theology:

> For Gebara it is this impulse to dominate and exploit in order to conquer want, imagining oneself to have transcended finite limitations, that has created the system of distortion that heaps excessive want and untimely death on the majority of humans. This system of exploitation threatens to undo the processes that maintain the life cycle of all earth beings in relation to one another, crafted by the earth over billions of years. It is this system of domination and distortion which is sin, as distinct from tragedy and death, which are natural and inevitable.¹⁰

Relationship is of the utmost importance in ecofeminism, and Gebara reconstructs an image of the Trinity that is not about metaphysics but *interrelationship*.¹¹ Gebara will expand traditional Trinitarian theology, giving it a dearly needed feminist flavor and stressing the relationships among poor women with a cosmological bent, reminding us of the Triune God's creative and life-giving presence in the entire universe. Sorrow, suffering, and death mysteriously coexist in interrelationship with joy, hope, and life—the hymn of the cosmos to the Holy Trinity. Since God chooses the poor of the earth and poor Mother Earth, the community that follows Jesus makes the same option for the poor and for creation. They are integrally interrelated. Special sensitivity to relationship leads us away from metaphysical preoccupation, anthropocentrism, dualism, oppression of the poor, women, earth, and creation, away from promises of illusory utopia, to the life of abundance in a real Paradise, hoped for in the risen Christ but present to us, in life-giving communion with God and one another, here and now.¹²

---

8. Gebara, *Longing for Running Waters*.
9. Ruether, *Christianity and Ecofeminism*, 103.
10. Ibid., 105–106.
11. Ibid, 107. Also Gebara, *El Nuevo Rostro de Dios*.
12. Eastern Orthodox Archpriest John Strickland has developed a series of podcasts, still incomplete, entitled *Paradise and Utopia*, in which he speaks

All Creation Groans

Leonardo Boff has also written extensively about the importance of ecological questions and their integral connection with poverty and injustice, faith and theology. He did his doctoral studies in Germany and has taught theology for many years in his native Brazil, where he also works with the base ecclesial communities. He is widely considered, along with Gustavo Gutiérrez, OP, a founder of liberation theology in Latin America. His first major work was a Christology from the perspective of the Latin American poor.[13] He has also treated ecclesiology[14] and published a number of books co-authored with his brother Clodovis.[15] Most recently, he has written essays about Pope Francis and continues to make connections between care for the poor, the environment, and theology. He has been associated with the Franciscans for many years.

Like Gebara, Boff sees an integral connection between the oppression of the poor and Mother Earth. A summary of his "ecotheology" can be found in *Cry of the Earth, Cry of the Poor*.[16] Boff says that until we see Mother Earth as a living organism to be respected and protected (he cites, among many others, biologist James Lovelock's work on the living earth as *Gaia*), we will continue to exploit her natural resources, which the powerful and wealthy of the world consider economic capital to be bought, sold, and exploited on the market.[17] A new respect for the Mother who

---

of "the rise and fall of Christendom." In these presentations, he stresses the importance of the centrality of Paradise, which he defines as "communion with God." Paradise stands at the center of the proclamation of the good news, in contrast to human-constructed "utopias." It should be noted that a number of Latin American theologians use the word "utopia" theologically much like Strickland uses "Paradise." I am grateful to Mother Melania of the faculty of Patriarch Athenagoras Orthodox Institute at Graduate Theological Union in Berkeley, CA, for recommending Fr. Strickland's podcasts. See http://www.ancientfaith.com/podcasts/paradiseutopia/post_christian_christendom.

13. See *Jesus Christ Liberator*.

14. See especially *Ecclesiogenesis*.

15. Among others, *Salvation and Liberation*, *Liberation Theology*, and *Introducing Liberation Theology*.

16. Boff, *Cry of the Earth, Cry of the Poor*.

17. Ibid., 15–20.

cares for us and gives us nourishment is required if humanity as a species is to survive. We belong to Mother Earth, herself a part of the solar system, the Milky Way galaxy, and the ever-expanding universe, all of which, along with our humanity, is enfolded into the loving arms of the Triune God, ultimate Creator and Sustainer. Care for oppressed Mother Earth requires a corresponding care for the poor. The only viable possibility for humanity is to move from the paradigm of conquest and domination to a new paradigm of care and mercy.[18] We must care for Mother Earth and the entire cosmos *because* we are human and self-conscious part of the cosmos. Among all creatures, we are given the ability to *reflect* on our place in the cosmos. The human being is conscious and has consciousness.[19] At the same time, it is essential for humanity to have a deep sense of the inter-connectedness of all creation.[20] The ecological crisis has come about because of the loss of this sense of inter-connectedness.[21] The human being manifests the shadow side of Western Civilization in the urge toward conquest, domination, and the priority of the self. Amazonia is an example of how the poor and creation are ruthlessly exploited, says Boff, a microcosm of the paradigm of conquest and domination. In the thirst for dominating and exploiting people, animals, vegetation, forests, and natural resources for the economic gain of a very few, the world's "largest natural reserve" has been decimated:

> The Amazon is the place where Gaia displays the lush riches of her body; it is also where she suffers the greatest violence. If we want to see the brutal face of the capitalist and industrial system, we need only visit the Brazilian Amazon. That is where all the capital sins (mortal sins and sins of capital) are committed. There we see in unvarnished form the pursuit of bigness by the spirit of modernity, the rationalizing of the irrational, and the crystal-clear logic of the system. We likewise witness the

18. Ibid., 7–15.
19. Ibid., 57.
20. Ibid., 58.
21. Ibid., 63–85.

clear contradiction between capitalism and ecology. To add the prefix *eco* to capitalism or to development projects—ecocapitalism or ecodevelopment—simply masks the inherent perversity of capitalism and its development paradigm. The internal logic of the system suggests that there is no such thing as ecology, or, if it does exist, it must be rejected.[22]

Amazonia is a living microcosm of the poor of the world and Mother Earth. The Brazilian government and multinational companies "have given rise to what has been called 'the Amazon mode of production.'"[23] Mother Earth and the poor suffer interminable violence, indigenous peoples are exterminated, and the poor are utilized as sheer labor to be exploited solely for personal and corporate economic gain. Amazonia illustrates how important it is for humankind to develop a "centrality of ecology" as a point of departure for stopping the repression and building a just society.[24]

Unless we integrate the wisdom of indigenous cultures, nature, and the best of Western art, science, and technology, humanity runs the grave risk of environmental catastrophe. It is imperative to stop the destruction. If Mother Earth is venerated and not exploited, if the poor are treated with dignity and their human rights respected, and, most especially, if we become aware of our deep connectedness with the Triune God, creation, and all our sisters and brothers, perhaps we will be able to arrest and reverse the destruction of the poor and Mother Earth. We will re-learn how to live in community with all life. This is the only way that humanity will be able to arrest the descending spiral of violence. In the meantime, the poor, as a result of the paradigm of domination, have become "the most threatened beings in creation."[25] Partnership should be actively pursued between liberation theology and

---

22. Ibid., 86.
23. Ibid.
24. Ibid.
25. Ibid., 110.

ecology, for to "hear the cry of the oppressed" is to attend to creation at its most basic level.[26]

What can the poor preaching Church do about this violence toward creation, Mother Earth, and the poor of the world? Boff gives us a clue. Education, he says, is *paramount* so that the human community can reverse the process:

> Having a new cosmology is not enough. How are we to spread it and bring people to internalize it so as to inspire new behaviors, nourish new dreams, and bolster a new kindness toward the Earth? That is certainly a pedagogical challenge. . . . [T]he new paradigm must form new kinds of subjectivity and enter into all realms of life, society, the family, the media, and educational institutions in order to show a new planetary man and woman, in cosmic solidarity and in tune with the overall direction of the evolutionary process.[27]

Given the possible destruction of all we hold dear, the Holy Preaching as proclamation on behalf of Mother Earth and the poor will be an indispensable service the preaching Church of the poor can provide for the world. An important part of this will be *formation*. I remind the reader of Bonhoeffer's *conformitas*. An ethical priority for him, it is today a task more important than ever. The Church community must be conformed to Jesus through education that respects the human being, the poor, and Mother Earth. This formation begins at the level of the local community. The poor are animated to assume their primary role as proclaimer of the Word. Boff gives a sense of what this will look like:

> The whole pedagogical process should culminate in such consciousness-raising, which confers on the human being, man and woman, a noble universal significance. Such consciousness-raising enables people to see clearly that the supreme and global value is to protect planet Earth (and with it the universe) and to safeguard those conditions that the planet has labored to build up for

26. Ibid., 104–14.
27. Ibid., 119.

All Creation Groans

fifteen billion years so that our life might maintain its inner tendency, which is self-actualization, reproduction, and progress, especially of human life.[28]

This formation will be a priority among pastoral agents working with the poor. In the Mexican immigrant community, it means giving pastoral theological education a primary role in preparing the preaching Church to assume its role as the proclaimer of justice. The Holy Preaching will take up Pope Francis' concern for the immigrant. This is already happening in the United States Catholic Conference of Bishops, who have, through Cardinal Sean O'Malley, organized celebrations of the Eucharist on the border of the United States and Mexico. The recent appointment of Archbishop Blase Cupich, a leading immigration rights and reform advocate, to the Archdiocese of Chicago, is also a hopeful sign. Pastoral agents, priests, and religious working in Mexican immigrant communities will become more committed to forming a poor preaching Church to proclaim prophetically the cry of justice to sisters and brothers in wealthier Church communities. A true solidarity will happen among local preaching Church communities, with a deeper sense of the importance of the immigrant in the global community and a knowledge of how immigration questions are integrally connected with the poor of the world, Mother Earth, and an entire universe in symphony with the Holy Trinity of life.

As the Apostle says, all creation groans in labor. The groaning of the poor preaching Church is the *Sacra Praedicatio*, the Holy Preaching. It, too, will help give birth to the New Creation, where poverty, injustice, and death no longer hold sway. The groan, the fruit of the Holy Spirit giving voice to the *pueblo*, rises up on behalf of Mother Earth, the universe, and the poor. The preaching Church is a hopeful people—the groans of labor become a joyful shout: Behold the New Child, the new creation held in the hands of the Triune God, Father-Mother, Son-Brother, Spirit of Life. Groan and shout are knit together in the community of the Holy Preaching, basking in the brilliant sunlight of the new creation.

---

28. Boff, *Cry of the Earth*, 122.

Conclusion

An "Ontonomy" of the Holy Preaching

At the beginning of this book in the Acknowledgements, I mentioned my long-time friend and mentor, Fr. John Heagle, who introduced me to the theology of Raimon Panikkar (1918–2010), a Catholic presbyter, philosopher, and theologian. A *peritus* at the Second Vatican Council, Panikkar helped write *Nostra Aetate*, the declaration on non-Christian faiths. Born on November 3, 1918, Panikkar's father was Hindu from India and his mother Catalonian Catholic. Ordained a Catholic presbyter for the Archdiocese of Barcelona, Spain, in 1946, he received his doctorate in philosophy, with additional doctorates in Science (University of Madrid, 1958) and Theology (Pontifical Lateran University, 1961). After acting as Visiting Professor at Harvard (1966), he studied Eastern philosophy and religion in India. From 1971–1987, he was professor of Comparative Religions at the University of California in Santa Barbara. In 1987, he returned to his native Catalonia, where he continued to teach, write, and study. He died in 2010.[1]

Panikkar's theology provides a good conclusion to a book dedicated to the preaching Church of the poor. He was fond of new words through which he expressed fresh realities, and

---

1. From Raimon Panikkar official site, (http://www.raimon-panikkar.org).

"ontonomy," one of his word inventions, best expresses what I have tried to say regarding the theology of preaching. I began with Dietrich Bonhoeffer, whose theology gives an insightful appreciation of the "Real." If Bonhoeffer stresses what is real in his theology, Panikkar invites a depth look at what he calls the "hidden" in the Real.[2] "Ontonomy" expresses being as an integral and undivided whole embracing *all reality*, including that which we cannot see, that which is "hidden," specifically, the divine. Ontonomy, unlike what Panikkar calls "heteronomy" (the traditional view) and "autonomy" (the modern view), allows for no split in reality; the other two, says Panikkar, are dualistic at core.[3] The theology of preaching has been overly influenced by dualisms: body and soul, flesh and spirit, material and spiritual, time and eternity, nature and grace, as well as many others that turn our theological reflection and praxis into neo-Platonic schizophrenia. Perhaps the most destructive two dualisms for preaching are those of rhetoric and theology, on the one hand, and preacher and individual on the other. The rhetoric of preaching is separated from theology at its peril; and preaching that divides the individual from the community stands in danger of annihilation. To this end, I have presented what is, in my opinion, a more holistic theology of preaching that speaks of the Holy Preaching in St. Dominic of Guzman's categories; that is, the Holy Preaching is primarily a living *community*, the people of God, the "living Christ walking among the people"—a preaching Church of the poor, the "voice" of the Holy Spirit. Perhaps the word "ontonomy" provides the surest way for the Holy Preaching to be real within the hidden and hidden within the Real.

In a short video about Raimon Panikkar that has been posted on the Internet, there is a section in which Panikkar himself speaks, using what he calls the "metaphor of the window."[4] He says that all of us see things through our own window; that is the only "reality" we see. But my sister and my brother see through another window to which I only have access through *their* eyes. To begin

2. Panikkar, *Worship and Secular Man*, 41.
3. Ibid., 28–29.
4. http://www.youtube.com/watch?v=1e0Sg3hMups.

An "Ontonomy" of the Holy Preaching

to understand what they see through their window, I must listen to the words that *they* speak. Then I can tell them about what it is that I see through my window, and there is dialogue. Hearing their word about what they see expands my own reality. A world community practicing the discipleship of the "window of the other" comes to a much broader view of reality through the insight of others. The *word of the other* is necessary for the integrity of my view, becoming wholeness and unity within the community.

Could this be a metaphor for the theology of preaching now and in the future? The Holy Preaching can never exist apart, by itself, simply words of the preacher separate from the community. It is, rather, an ontonomy of words that becomes part of the cosmos of dialogue in the Holy Preaching that is the people of God, especially "hidden" in the community of the preaching Church of the poor.

For Panikkar, there is an integral relationship between Silence and the Word.[5] In turn, silence and word are an integral part of *being*. They form a non-dualistic whole. He quotes Wis 18:14–15: "For while gentle silence enveloped all things . . . Your all-powerful word leaped from heaven." Silence "is a kind of 'property' of Being prior to Being."[6] Although we make distinctions between silence and being, they cannot be severed, separated, or divided from one another.[7] God is *known* in stillness, in silence, and silence is an integral part of being. As silence forms a part of Being, so does the Word. "Silence," says Panikkar, "is not the negation of Being; it is not Non-Being." But he continues:

> Silence . . . is the absence of everything, and ultimately an absence of Being. It is anterior, prior to Being. Silence in this sense of absence of Being is closer to the Spanish *nada* . . . than to the English "nothingness." In a word, to become aware of the silence of Being and the silence of the word is close to discovering the divine dimension.

---

5. Panikkar, *The Rhythm of Being*, 323–41.
6. Ibid., 323.
7. Ibid., 324.

Part Three: Among

... Words began in silence. They are not separate from silence.[8]

For the theology of preaching, the word and silence are necessary for dialogue, for conversation, the root meaning of homily. When we speak, we use the word, and when we listen, we are silent. Speaking and listening are done *intentionally*. Silence and word leap forth in the creative being that is intentional dialogue, and intentional dialogue is the mid-wife in the birth of the Holy Preaching. Preaching as the action of speaking is not done in a vacuum, preacher and pulpit hermetically sealed from the community of life. The Word is listened to in the active silence of the conversation partner; and the "silent listening" of the partner becomes "active word" in dialogue. The active word is dialogic with *active* silent listening. Neither is passive. They are united in an ontonomy of praxis. For those who follow Jesus, praxis of discipleship defines *who* the community of the Holy Preaching really is:

> All our talk about Silence proves that Silence is never alone. . . . Silence needs the word in order to be silence. . . . This Silence belongs to the divine dimension, but it needs the word or rather it is not without the word. Silence has no expression, or rather it begets the expression, the Language, the Word, the Logos. . . . The awareness of being begotten by the word is perhaps our highest dignity, since it brings us in touch with the most conspicuous divine dimension. We are born of the word and thus share the nature of the word. . . . The Word is a divine dimension of the real. To truly speak is to be in touch with this divine dimension. . . . When Silence and Word are kept separate, the Silence is terrifying and the Word ceases to be "Word of God," becoming only our words about God; theo-logy loses its sacredness . . . and becomes our scrutiny of the Inscrutable. . . . This divine dimension of the ordinary word is not always conspicuous in the speaker or conscious in the listener. . . . In language, the human and the divine worlds communicate,

---

8. Ibid., 325, 333.

An "Ontonomy" of the Holy Preaching

each in its proper way.... [T]he Divine and the Human share in the Word.[9]

Worship and prayer emerge from this creative dialogue. The act of preaching is a formal part of Christian worship, but it must go hand and hand with the *praxis* of the community, the poor preaching Church, in what Panikkar calls "doing."[10] Silence, Word, Being, our human words, our communication, all are intimately inter-related in an ontonomic *perichoeresis* that reflects the divine presence of the Trinity in the community of the Holy Preaching.[11] The Triune God, for Panikkar, is the foundation of *all* reality. In commenting on Panikkar's vision of the Holy Trinity, Francis X. D'Sa, SJ, says: "God is Silence total and absolute, the silence of Being—and not only the being of silence. His word, who completely expresses and consumes him, is the Son. The *Father has* no being, the Son is *his* being.... The Spirit ... is the We of the Trinity."[12] In this *perichoeresis*, the Father is Silence, the Son is Word, and the Spirit is We. Silence, Word, and We have their *oikonomia* in the Holy Preaching, in the preaching Church of the poor, in the icon of the Trinity that is the Church community.

However, the poor preaching Church is actually more than icon; it is the *presence* of the economic Holy Trinity in perichoeretic praxis through the words of the Holy Preaching. The Trinitarian structure, for Panikkar, is so deeply rooted in reality that it *is* reality[13]—an ontonomy with no room for dualistic thinking. "All things," says Panikkar, "are ... in fact, trinitarian."[14] Trinitarian *perichoeresis* permeates all that is Real. It is a hidden presence, a *Deus absconditus*. Words reveal and hide the presence of the Trinity. A primary task, then, of the preaching Church is to assure that words are used carefully for the revelation of all that is Real. The

---

9. Ibid., 337, 340–41.
10. Ibid., 349–53.
11. Ibid., 321, 329.
12. D'Sa, "The Notion of God," 40.
13. Panikkar, *The Cosmotheandirc Experience*, 55.
14. Ibid., 60.

hidden poor in our midst are gifted with special *locus* by the Triune God. They reflect the privileged *perichoeresis* of the creative *oikonomia*, the preaching center at the heart of the praxis of the living God. The Sacramental Word is emptied of riches and fame, prestige and power. The presence of the living Christ walks among the *pueblo*, the voice of the Spirit resounds in weakness, and the Holy Preaching, the preaching Church of the poor, is enfleshed in the vulnerable Word community.

References Cited

Acevedo, Marcelo de C., SJ. *Basic Ecclesial Communities in Brazil: The Challenge of a New Way of Being Church*. Washington D.C.: Georgetown University Press, 1987.

Augustine of Hippo. "Sermon 272 on the Eucharist." http://www.earlychurchtexts.com/public/augustine_sermon_272_eucharist.htm

Barreiro, Alvaro, SJ. *Basic Ecclesial Communities: The Evangelization of the Poor*. Maryknoll, NY: Orbis, 1982.

Barth, Karl. *Homiletics*. Louisville: Westminster John Knox, 1991.

———. *Prayer: Fiftieth Anniversary Edition*. Edited by Don E. Saliers. From the translation of Sara F. Terrien. With Essays by I. John Hesselink, Daniel L. Migliore, and Donald K. McKim. Louisville:Westminster John Knox, 2002.

Baum, Gregory, ed. *The Twentieth Century: A Theological Overview*. Maryknoll, NY: Orbis, 1999.

Boff, Leonardo. *Christianity in a Nutshell*. Translated by Phillip Berryman. Maryknoll, NY: Orbis, 2013.

———. *Cry of the Earth, Cry of the Poor*. Translated by Phillip Berryman. Maryknoll, NY: Orbis, 1997.

———. *Ecclesiogenesis: The Base Communities Reinvent the Church*. Translated by Robert R. Barr. Maryknoll, NY: Orbis, 1986.

———. *Jesus Christ Liberator: A Critical Theology for Our Time*. Translated by Patrick Hughes. Maryknoll, NY: Orbis, 1978.

———. *The Lord's Prayer: The Prayer of Integral Liberation*. Translated by Theodore Morrow. Maryknoll, NY: Orbis, 1983.

———. *New Evangelization: Good News to the Poor*. Translated by Robert Barr. Eugene, OR: Wipf and Stock, 2006.

———. *Passion of Christ, Passion of the World*. Maryknoll, NY: Orbis, 2011.

Boff, Leonardo and Clodovis Boff. *Introducing Liberation Theology*. Maryknoll, NY: Orbis, 1987.

———. *Liberation Theology: From Dialog to Confrontation*. San Francisco: Harper and Row, 1986.

———. *Salvation and Liberation*. Maryknoll, NY: Orbis, 1984.

References Cited

Bonhoeffer, Dietrich. *Dietrich Bonhoeffer Works*. Volumes 1—17. Edited by Victoria Barnett, Clifford Green, et al. Minneapolis: Fortress Press, 1996—2014.

———. *Dietrich Bonhoeffer Werke*. Bänder 1–17 und Engänzungsbänder. München: Christian Kaiser, 1986–1999.

Brock, Sebastian. *The Luminous Eye: The Spiritual World Vision of Saint Ephrem*. Kalamazoo: Cistercian, 1992.

Cardenal, Ernesto. *The Gospel in Solentiname*. Fifth Edition. Maryknoll, NY: Orbis, 2010.

Carroll, James. *Constantine's Sword*. First Run Feature Films, 2007.

Case-Winters, Anna. *Reconstructing a Christian Theology of Nature: Down to Earth*. Hampshire, UK: Ashgate, 2007.

Catechism of the Catholic Church. No. 1128. http://www.vatican.va/archive/ccc_css/archive/catechism/p2s1c1a2.htm, February 23, 2015.

Catherine of Siena. *The Dialogue*. Translation and Introduction by Suzanne Noffke, OP, Preface by Giuliana Cavallini. New York: Paulist, 1980.

Chauvet, Louis-Marie, OP. *The Sacraments: The Word of God at the Mercy of the Body*. Collegeville, MN: Liturgical, 2001.

Codina, Víctor, SJ. *Los Caminos del Oriente Cristiano: Una Iniciación a la Teología Oriental*. Santander: Sal Terrae, 1997.

———. *Creo en el Espíritu Santo*. Santander: Sal Terrae, 1994.

———. *El Espíritu del Señor Actúa desde Abajo*. Santander: Sal Terrae, 2015.

———. *No Extingáis el Espíritu: Una Inciación a la Pnuematología*. Santander: Sal Terrae, 2008.

———. *Para Comprender la Eclesiología desde América Latina*. Nueva Edición Renovada. Santander: Sal Terrae, 2008.

———. *Renacer a la Solidaridad*. Santander: Sal Terrae, 1982.

———. "Sacraments." In *Systematic Theology: Perspectives from Liberation Theology*. Edited by Jon Sobrino and Ignacio Ellacuría. Maryknoll, NY: Orbis, 1996.

Comblin, José. *The Holy Spirit and Liberation*. Translated by Paul Burns. Eugene, OR: Wipf and Stock, 2004.

———. *Tiempo de Acción: Ensayo sobre el Espíritu y la Historia*. Lima: Centro de Estudios y Publicaciones, 1986.

———. *La Vida: En Búsqueda de la Libertad*. Santiago: Movimiento Teología de la Liberación, 2008.

Consemius, Victor. "The Condemnation of Modernism and the Survival of Catholic Theology." In *The Twentieth Century: A Theological Overview*. Edited by Gregory Baum. Maryknoll, NY: Orbis, 1999.

Corbon, Jean, OP. *The Wellspring of Worship*. Translated by Matthew J. O'Connell. New York: Paulist, 1988.

Dalton, Anne Marie, and Henry C. Simmons. *Ecology and the Practice of Hope*. Albany, NY: State University of New York Press, 2010.

De Lange, Frits. *Waiting for the Word: Dietrich Bonhoeffer on Speaking about God*. Translated by Martin N. Walton. Grand Rapids: Eerdmans, 1999.

References Cited

De Las Casas, Bartolome. *The History of the Indies.* Translated and Edited by A. Collard. New York: Harper and Row, 1971.

De Santa Ana, Julio. *Good News to the Poor: The Challenge of the Poor in the History of the Church.* Geneva: World Council of Churches, 1977.

Doblmeier, Martin. *Bonhoeffer: Pastor, Pacifist, Nazi Resister.* Journey Films, 2003.

D'Sa, Francis Xavier. SJ. "The Notion of God," in *The Intercultural Challenge of Raimon Panikkar.* Edited by Joseph Prabhu. Maryknoll, NY: Orbis, 1996.

Ebeling, Gerhard. *On Prayer: The Lord's Prayer in Today's World.* Philadelphia: Fortress, 1978.

Ellacuria, Ignacio, SJ. "The Crucified People," in *Mysterium Liberationis: Fundamental Concepts of Liberation Theology.* Edited by Jon Sobrino, SJ, and Ignacio Ellacuria, SJ. Maryknoll, NY: Orbis, 2004.

Ephrem the Syrian. *Hymns: The Classics of Western Spirituality.* Translated and Introduced by Kathleen E. McVey. Preface by John Meyendorff. New York: Paulist, 1989.

Evagrius of Pontus. *The Greek Ascetic Corpus.* Tranlated with Introduction and Commentary by Robert E. Sinkewicz. New York: Oxford University Press. 2006.

Fant, Clyde E. *Bonhoeffer: Worldly Preaching.* New York: Thomas Nelson, 1975.

———. *Preaching for Today.* New York: Harper and Row, 1987.

Florence, Anna Carter. *Preaching as Testimony.* Louisville: Westminster John Knox, 2007.

Forde, Gerhard O. *Theology is for Proclamation.* Minneapolis: Fortress, 1990.

Forte, Bruno. *La Iglesia, Icono de la Trinidad: Breve Eclesiología.* Tercer Edición. Tradujo Alfonso Ortíz García. Salamanca: Sígueme, 2003.

Garibay Gómez, Javier. *Nepantla, Situados en Medio: Estudio Histórico-Teológico de la Realidad Indiana.* México, D.F.: Centro de Reflexión Teológica, 2000.

Garrison, Becky. *Red and Blue God, Black and Blue Church: Eyewitness Accounts of How American Churches are Hijacking Jesus, Bagging the Beatitudes, and Worshiping the Almighty Dollar.* San Francisco: Jossey-Bass, 2006.

Gebara, Ivone. *Longing for Running Water: Ecofemisim and Liberation.* Minneapolis: Fortress, 1999.

———. *El Nuevo Rostro de Dios: Una Reconstrucción de los Significados Trinitarios.* México, D.F.: Dabar, 1994.

———. "The Trinity and Human Experience: An Ecofeminist Approach." In *Women Healing Earth.* Edited by Rosemary Radford Ruether. Maryknoll, NY: Orbis, 1996.

Gonzalez Faus, José Ignacio, SJ. *Al Tercer Dia Resuscitó de entre los Muertos.* Madrid: PPC Comunicaciones, 2002.

Green, Clifford J. *Bonhoeffer: A Theology of Sociality.* Revised Edition. Grand Rapids: Eerdmans, 1999.

Green, Clifford J. And Michael P. DeJonge, eds. *The Bonhoeffer Reader.* Minneapolis: Fortress, 2013.

References Cited

Groody, Daniel G. and Gioacchino Campese, eds. *A Promised Land, A Perilous Journey: Theological Perspectives on Migration.* Notre Dame: University of Notre Dame Press, 2008.

Gutiérrez, Gustavo, OP. *En Busca de los Pobres de Jesucristo: El Pensamiento de Bartolomé de Las Casas* Lima: Centro de Estudios y Publicaciones, 1992.

———. *A Theology of Liberation: History, Politics, and Salvation.* Translated and Edited by Sister Caridad Inda and John Eagleson. Maryknoll, NY: Orbis, 1973.

Hammerling, Roy. *The Lord's Prayer in the Early Church: The Pearl of Great Price.* New York: Palgrave MacMillan, 2010.

Handel, George Friedrich. *Dixit Dominus.* http://imslp.org/wiki/Dixit_Dominus,_HWV_232_(Handel,_George_Frideric).

Heille, Gregory, OP, ed. *Theology of Preaching: Essays and Vision and Ministry in the Pulpit.* London: Melisende, 2001.

Hesse, Dieter T. and Rosemary Radford Ruether, eds. *Christianity and Ecology: Seeking the Well-Being of Earth and Humans.* Cambridge, Mass: Harvard University Press, 2010.

Holbert, John C. *Preaching Creation: The Environment and the Pulpit.* Eugene, OR: Cascade, 2012.

Janowiak, Paul A., SJ. *The Holy Preaching: The Sacramentality of the Word in the Liturgical Assembly.* Collegeville, MN: Liturgical, 2000.

———. "Running to Communion." *America* 189 (2003) 15—17.

———. *Standing Together in the Community of God: Liturgical Spirituality and the Presence of Christ.* Collegeville, MN: Liturgical, 2011.

Jenkins, Willis. *Ecologies of Grace: Environental Ethics and Christian Theology.* New York: Oxford University Press, 2008.

Jeremias, Joachim. *The Lord's Prayer.* Philadelphia: Fortress, 1969.

John Chrysostom. *On Wealth and Poverty.* Translated and Introduced by Catherine P. Roth. Crestwood, NY: St. Vladimir's Seminary Press, 1984.

Kadavil, Mathai. *The World as Sacrament: Sacramentality of Creation from the Perspectives of Leonardo Boff, Alexander Schmemann and Saint Ephrem.* Leuven: Peters, 2005.

Kelly, Geffrey B., ed. *Karl Rahner: Theologian of the Graced Search for Meaning.* Minneapolis: Fortress, 1992.

Kidder, Annemarie S. "Bonhoeffer in the Company of Martyrs: Rupert Mayer, SJ." Beeson Divinity School, Samford University. April 2013. https://www.youtube.com/watch?v=aQwYZ4qT50w.

LaCugna, Catherine Mowry. *God for Us: The Trinity and Christian Life.* San Francisco: Harper, 1993.

Lindsey, William D. "Interview with Ivone Gebara." August 28, 2013. http://bilgrimage.blogspot.com/2013/08/brazilian-theologian-ivone-gebara-on.html.

Lohfink, Gerhard. *Jesus and Community: The Social Dimension of Christian Faith.* Translated by John P. Galvin. Philadelphia: Fortress, 1984.

References Cited

Lorenz, Edward C., Dana E. Aspinall, J. Michael Raley, eds. *Montesinos' Legacy: Defining and Defending Human Rights for Five Hundred Years.* Lanham, MD: Lexington, 2014.

Marins, José. "Comunidades Eclesiais de Base na América Latina." *Concilium* 104 (1975) 20—29.

Marins, José F., Teolide M. Trevisan. *Fundamentalismos: Obsessão Contemporârea.* São Paulo: Pollatti. 2013.

McGrath, Alister E. http://www.alistermcgrathwiley.com/glossary.asp.

Migoya, Francisco, SJ. *El Jesuita que Se Enfrentó a Hitler.* México, D.F.: Buena Prensa, 2011.

Moltmann, Jürgen. *The Crucified God: The Cross of Christ as the Foundation and Criticism of Christian Theology.* Translated by R. A. Wilson and John Bowden. Minneapolis: Fortress, 1993.

Montes Lara, María Teresa, OP. "The Indigenous Face of God in the Mexican Immigrant Community: A Leadership Formation Proposal from the Pauline Ecclesiology of Baptism." DMin Thesis Project, Barry University, 2014.

Musto, Ronald G. *Liberation Theologies: A Research Guide.* New York: Garland, 1991.

Nessan, Craig L. *Orthopraxis or Heresy: The North American Theological Response to Latin American Liberation Theology.* Atlanta: Scholars, 1989.

New York Times. http://www.nytimes.com/2013/09/24/us/immigrant-population-shows-signs-of-growth-estimates-show.html?_r=0.

O'Driscoll, Mary, OP. "Catherine the Theologian." *Spirituality Today* 40 (1988), 4—17.

Orthodox Bishops of America. "On Preaching." https://oca.org/holy-synod/encyclicals/on-preaching.

Panikkar, Raimon. *Christophany: The Fullness of Man.* Translated by Alfred DiLascia. Maryknoll, NY: Orbis, 2004.

———. *Il Cristo Sconosciuto dell'Inuismo.* Milano: Vita e Pensiero, 1976.

———. *The Cosmotheandric Experience: Emerging Religious Consciousness.* Edited with Introduction by Scott Eastham. Maryknoll, NY: Orbis, 1993.

———. *The Intra-Religious Dialogue.* New York: Paulist, 1998.

———. "Metaphor of the Window." http://www.youtube.com/watch?v=1eoSg3hMups.

———. *Opera Omnia, Mysticism and Spirituality: Part Two, Spirituality, the Way of Life.* Volumes One and Two. Edited by Milena Carrara Pavan. Maryknoll, NY: Orbis, 2014.

———. *The Rhythm of Being: The Gifford Lectures.* Maryknoll, NY: Orbis, 2010.

———. *The Silence of God: The Answer of the Buddha.* Translated by Robert R. Barr. Maryknoll, NY: Orbis, 1989.

———. *Worship and Secular Man: A Study Towards an Integral Anthropology.* London: Darton, Longman, and Todd. 1972.

Pastro, Vincent J. *Enflamed by the Sacramental Word: Preaching and the Imagination of the Poor.* Eugene, OR: Pickwick, 2010.

References Cited

Peñalosa, Joaquin Antonio. *Manual de la Imperfecta Homilía*, Quinta Edición. México, D.F.: Buena Prensa, 2004.

Pew Research Center, April 2012. http://pewresearch.org/pubs/2250/mexican-immigration-immigrants-illegal-border-enforcement-deportations-migration-flows.

Pieris, Aloysius, SJ. *An Asian Theology of Liberation*. Maryknoll, NY: Orbis, 1988.

Pobee, John S. *Who are the Poor? The Beatitudes as a Call to Community*. Geneva: WCC, 1987.

Prabhu, Joseph, ed. *The Intercultural Challenge of Raimon Panikkar*. Maryknoll, NY: Orbis, 1996.

Public Broadcast Station. http://www.pbs.org/itvs/beyondtheborder/immigration.html.

Rahner, Karl, SJ. *Foundations of Christian Faith: An Introduction to the Idea of Christianity*. Translated by William V. Dych. New York: Seabury, 1978.

———. Encounters with Silence. Translated by James M. Demske, SJ. Westminster, MD: Newman, 1962.

———. *Spirit in the World*. Forward by Johannes Baptist Metz. New York: Bloomsbury Academic, 1994.

Raimon Panikkar Official Site. http://www.raimon-panikkar.org.

Raya, Joseph. *The Transfiguration of Our Lord and Savior Jesus Christ*. Combermere, ON: Madonna, 1992.

Resner, André. *Preacher and Cross: Person and Message in Theology and Rhetoric*. Grand Rapids: Eerdmans, 1999.

Rondet, Michel. *La Trinidad Narrada*. Traducido por Ramon Alfonso Díez Aragón. Santander: Sal Terrae, 2008.

Ruether, Rosemary Radford, ed. *Women Healing Earth: Third World Woman on Ecology, Feminism, and Religion*. Maryknoll, NY: Orbis, 1996.

Scannone, Juan Carlos, SJ. *Religión y Nuevo Pensamiento: Hacía una Filosofía de la Religión para Nuestro Tiempo para América Latina*. Barcelona: Anthropos, 2005.

Schmemann, Alexander. *For the Life of the World: Sacraments and Orthodoxy*. Crestwood, NY: St. Vladimir's Seminary Press, 1973.

Schillebeeckx, Edward, OP. *Christ the Sacrament of the Encounter with God*. New York: Sheed and Ward, 1987.

———. *The Schillebeeckx Reader*. Edited by Robert Schreiter. New York: Crossroad, 1984.

Seasoltz, R. Kevin, OSB, ed. *Living Bread, Saving Cup*. Expanded Edition. Collegeville: Liturgical, 1982.

Segundo, Juan Luis, SJ. *A Theology for Artisans of a New Humanity: The Sacraments Today*. Volume 4. Translated by John Drury. Maryknoll, NY: Orbis, 1974.

Silvas, Anna M. *The Asketikon of St Basil the Great*. New York: Oxford University Press, 2005.

References Cited

Sobrino, Jon. *Christology at the Crossroads.* Translated by John Drury. Maryknoll, NY: Orbis, 1979.

———. *Jesus the Liberator: A Historical-Theological View.* Translated by Paul Burns and Francis McDonogh. Maryknoll, NY: Orbis, 1993.

———. *The Principle of Mercy: Taking the Crucified People from the Cross.* Maryknoll, NY: Orbis, 1994.

———. *The True Church and the Poor.* Translated by Matthew J. O'Connell. Maryknoll, NY: Orbis, 1984.

Strickland, John, "Paradise and Utopia." http://www.ancientfaith.com/podcasts/paradiseutopia/post_christian_christendom.

Tamez, Elsa, ed. *Through Her Eyes: Women's Theology from Latin America.* Maryknoll, NY: Orbis, 1989.

Taylor, Barbara Brown. *When God Is Silent.* Cambridge, MA: Crowley, 1998.

Todt, Heinz Eduard. *Authentic Faith: Bonhoeffer's Theological Ethics in Context.* Grand Rapids: Eerdmans, 2007.

Torres, Valerie. "La Familia as Locus Theologicus and Religious Education in Lo Cotidiano." *Religious Education* 105 (2010) 444—61.

Vassar University. http://vq.vassar.edu/issues/2012/02/vassar-today/at-the-border-nation-god-and-human-rights.html.

White, C. Vanessa. "The Holy Spirit in the Acts of the Apostles: A Pentecost Spirituality." *Bible Today* 52 (2014) 140—146.

Wingren, Gustaf. *The Living Word: A Theological Study of Preaching and the Church.* Translated by Victor C. Pogue. Philadelphia: Fortress, 1960.

Wright, N.T. *The Lord and His Prayer.* Grand Rapids: Eerdmans, 1997.

Name Index

A
Acevedo, Marcelo, 114–15, 143
Adam, 23, 86
Afanasiev, Nicolas, 90
Antonio de Montesinos, 22–24, 53, 104–106, 112
Arias Montes, Manuel, 79
Augustine of Hippo, St., 23, 49, 70, 143
Azariah, 123

B
Barreiro, Alvaro, 113–114, 143
Barth, Karl, xiv, 7, 17, 24, 37, 78, 85, 89, 121, 143
Bartolomé de Las Casas, 15, 23, 29, 105–106, 113, 145, 146
Basil the Great, St., xii, 67, 148
Boff, Clodovis, 131, 143
Boff, Leonardo, xiv, 1, 31–32, 33, 45, 59, 76–77, 78, 82, 97, 109, 111, 115, 117, 120, 121, 128, 131–35, 143, 146
Bonhoeffer, Dietrich, xi, xiv, 5, 6, 10, 11–28, 31, 41, 43, 49, 53–54, 55, 64, 65, 78, 82–83, 86, 91, 93–94, 105, 107, 116, 126, 134, 138, 144, 145, 146, 149
Brock, Sebastian, 89, 144
Burns, Thomas, 127
Buttrick, David, 2

C
Caldas, Carlos, xiv
Callahan, Sharon, xiv
Cappadocians, xii, 63
Cardenal, Ernesto, 23, 58, 144
Case-Winters, Anna, 128, 144
Catherine of Alexandria, St., xii, 7
Catherine of Siena, St., 42–43, 89, 144
Codina, Víctor, xiv, 47, 59, 90–91, 144
Comblin, José, 57, 63, 65, 71, 87, 106, 124, 144
Craddock, Fred, 2
Cumaru, Luis, xiv
Cupich, Blase, 135

D
Dalton, Anne Marie, 129, 144
David (King), 123
De Lange, Fritz, 11, 13, 54, 144
Diego de Colón, 23
Dominic of Guzman, St., 6, 15, 62, 97, 111, 138
D'Sa, Francis Xavier, 141, 145

E
Ebeling, Gerhard, 78, 145
Eldad and Medad, 123
Ellacuría, Ignacio, 34, 144, 145
Ephrem the Syrian, St., 7, 53, 67, 89, 144, 145, 146

Name Index

Evdokimov, Paul, xiv, 90

F
Fant, Clyde E., 7, 11–15, 19, 22, 24, 145
Fernandez, Eddie, xiv
Figueroa Deck, Alan, 115, 124
Florence, Anna Carter, 12, 145
Forte, Bruno, 52, 63, 119, 145

G
Garibay, Javier, 40, 41, 145
Gebara, Ivone, xiv, 69, 118, 128–131, 145, 146
Gonzalez Faus, José Ignacio, 124, 145
Green, Clifford, 5, 78, 83, 144, 145
Gregory of Nyssa, St., xii, 7, 67, 78
Gregory Palamas, St., 54
Gutiérrez, Gustavo, 3, 15, 29, 61, 72, 82, 90, 117, 131, 146

H
Händel, Georg Friedrich, 51
Heagle, John, xiv, 137
Heille, Gregory, xiv, 28, 32, 60, 88, 146
Hunthausen, Raymond G., 5

I
Ignatius of Loyola, St., 87
Irenaeus of Lyons, St., 87, 124
Ituarte, Gonzalo, 23, 58, 111

J
Jahziel, 123
Janowiak, Paul, xiv, 6, 61–62, 65, 146
Jeremias, Joachim, 77–79, 122, 146
Joel (the Prophet), 123
John Chrysostom, St., 21, 23, 68, 69, 83, 86, 162
John the Baptist, St., 22–23
John of the Cross, St., 89
John the Evangelist, St., 52

John Paul II, St., 84–85
John XXIII, St., 7
Josephus, 64

K
Kadavil, Mathai, 45, 146
Kidder, Annemarie S., 126, 146
Küng, Hans, 5, 12

L
LaCugna, Catherine Mowry, xiv, 63, 146
Lazarus, 67, 72
Levinas, Emmanuel, 116
Lohfink, Gerhard, 81–82, 146
Lorenz, Edward, 104, 147
Lossky, Vladimir, 90
Lowry, Eugene, 2

M
Macrina the Elder, St., xii
Macrina the Younger, St., xii, 7
Marins, José, xiv, 5, 15, 23, 38, 58, 71, 119, 120, 147
Marx, Karl, 26
Massaro, Thomas, xiv
Maximus Confessor, St., 53, 78
Mayer, Rubert, Bl., 125–26
McDonnell, Killian, 92
Melania, Mother, 131
Melania of Egypt, St., xii
Meyendorff, John, xiv, 145
Micah (the Prophet), 123
Migoya, Francisco, 125, 147
Miriam, 55
Moltmann, Jürgen, 32, 147
Montes Lara, María Teresa, x, xv, 71
Moses, 55, 100
Murphy-O'Conner, Jerome, 49

N
Nissiotis, Nikos, 90

O
Olympias, St., xii

Name Index

O'Malley, Sean, 135
Origen, 67

P
Panikkar, Raimon, xi, xiii, xiv, xv, 40, 41–42, 59, 63–66, 90, 116, 137–42, 145, 147, 148
Patriarch Bartholomew, 83–83
Paul of Tarsus, St., 41, 43, 49, 57, 65, 91
Pedro de Córdoba, 23, 105, 106, 112
Pelikan, Jaroslav, xii
Peñalosa, Joaquin Antonio, 126, 148
Perpetua and Felicity, Sts., ix–xii,
Pham, Hung, xiv
Pope Benedict XVI, 68
Pope Francis, 5, 8, 19, 68, 69, 74, 75, 79, 83, 84, 90, 94, 100, 101, 108, 109, 110, 116, 131, 135

Q
Quickley, George, xiv

R
Rahner, Karl, xiv, 5, 10, 45, 47, 54, 55, 87, 112, 114, 121, 124, 126, 148
Raya, Joseph, 52, 148
Resner, André, 126, 148
Romero, Oscar, Bl., 28
Ruether, Rosemary Radford, 128, 130, 145, 146, 148
Ruggere, Peter, xiv
Ruiz, Samuel, 58

S
Scannone, Juan Carlos, 74, 116, 148

Schillebeeckx, Edward, xiv, 9–10, 15, 17, 45, 47, 50, 109, 114, 148
Schleiermacher, Friedrich Daniel Ernst, 37
Schmemann, Alexander, 45, 90, 146, 148
Seasoltz, Kevin, 46, 49, 148
Segundo, Juan Luis, xiv, 73–74, 148
Semmelroth, Otto, xiv, 5–6, 47, 65
Simmons, Henry, 129, 144
Sobrino, Jon, 27, 28, 31, 33, 50, 81, 144, 145, 149
Saul (King), 123

T
Tamez, Elsa, 129, 149
Taylor, Barbara Brown, 2, 5, 125, 149
Teresa of Avila, St., 89
Thecla, St., xii
Thomas Aquinas, St., 15, 46, 54, 121, 124
Tödt, Heinz Eduard, 21, 149
Torres, Gilmer, 34
Torres, Valerie, 60, 149
Trevisan, Teolide María, xv, 147

V
Von Döllinger, Ignaz, 37
Von Harnack, Adolf, 37

W
Williams, Tamara, xiv
Wingren, Gustaf, 12, 149
Wright, N. T., 78, 82, 149

Z
Zechariah, 123
Zerubbabel, 123

Subject Index

A
"*Advaita*" ("creative polarities"), 40, 41–44
Alter Christus, 65
Amazonia, 131–32
Atonement (Satisfaction) theory of redemption, 32–33, 35
Autonomy, 138

B
Baptism, 12, 17, 27, 41, 48, 69, 77, 78, 114, 147
  commitment of, 1, 70, 124
  preachers by, x, 1–9, 12, 71, 78
  priests by, 1, 2
"Big Bang," 122
Border
  Mexico – U.S., 19, 28–29, 72, 102–3, 105, 135
  "Sunday," 29

C
Catequesis Familiar, 114
Capitalism, 36, 133
CELAM, see also "*Medellín*," "*Puebla*," 113
"Christic experience," 64–66
Christus Praesens, 13–15, 23
Church, xiii, 3, 4, 5, 6, 14, 17, 19, 22, 24, 25, 31, 35, 41, 44, 46, 47, 48, 49, 50, 54, 61, 62, 66, 68, 69, 73, 74, 87, 95, 100, 108, 109, 111, 113, 114, 121
Christ, body of, 5, 7, 12, 14, 15, 24, 34, 43, 49–50, 57, 71, 87, 91, 94–95, 108, 124
Church community, 3, 5, 6, 10, 12, 13, 14, 15, 19, 24, 28, 39, 43, 44, 45, 47, 48, 49, 50, 52, 55, 62, 63, 65–67, 69, 73, 75, 85, 87, 88, 91, 98, 100, 103, 107, 108, 111, 119, 120, 121, 124, 125, 134, 135, 137
Church as Person (Bonhoeffer), 65, 107
Church as Sacrament, 3, 17, 40–41, 44, 45, 47, 48–50, 114, 119
Church of the poor, xv, 4, 7, 8, 10, 15, 16, 40, 58, 60, 69, 75, 78–79, 90–91, 94, 98, 105, 107, 108, 109, 111, 115, 117, 119, 121, 124, 125, 126, 127, 134, 135, 137–39, 141–42
colonial Church, 112–13
Communion of Saints (*sanctorum communio*), xiii, 62, 65, 66
Bonhoeffer dissertation, 5, 13–14
creation of the Holy Spirit, 5, 12, 14, 24, 43, 108, 124

Subject Index

Church *(continued)*
  early Church, 16–17, 45, 46, 77, 80
  Eastern Church, 48, 88–89, 121
  hierarchical Church, 69
  "icon of the Holy Trinity," see "Holy Trinity"
  institutional Church, 74, 88–89
  living Church, 90
  local Church as full expression of universal Church, see also "*comunidades eclesiales de base*," 119–20
  Mexican immigrant preaching community, x, 13, 15–16, 18–19, 28–30, 71, 99–107
  mission Church, ix, 94, 115, 124
  North American Church, 38–39, 71
  New Testament Church, 122–23
  Orthodox Church, 2, 48, 74, 88, 90, 93, 95, 113, 121, 130, 131
  people of God, ix–x, 1, 4–7, 12, 14, 32, 43, 52, 65, 66, 68, 81–82, 93, 94, 97–98, 108, 123, 124, 138, 139
  preaching Church, ix, xv, 4, 5, 6, 7, 10, 28, 29, 31, 35, 40, 41, 44, 49, 52, 54, 55, 57, 58, 59, 60, 65, 66, 67, 69, 71, 74, 75, 76, 78, 80, 82, 84, 85, 86, 88, 90, 91, 93, 94, 95, 96, 97, 100, 103, 105, 107, 109, 111, 115, 117, 119, 120, 121, 124, 125, 126, 127, 128, 134, 135, 137, 139, 141, 142
  Reformation Church, 48
  Roman Catholic Church, 68, 73, 110, 121
  sacrament of Christ, 17, 45, 48, 50, 106, 119
  universal Church, 98, 108–9, 119–20
  wealthy Church, 109, 115, 135
  western Church, 88–89
Colonial presence in Latin America, genocide and religious results, 112–13
Comunidades eclesiales de base ("Base ecclesial communities"), xv, 5, 19, 24, 58, 74, 100, 106–7, 109, 111, 113–15, 119–20, 129, 131
Contemplata aliis trader, 126
Conversion (*Metanoia*), 25, 71, 113, 114, 125
Cosmos, 34, 47, 50, 61, 66, 77, 78, 80, 81, 83, 127–35
Cross, 16, 26–35, 112
  as consequence of commitment to poor, 32–35
  as "pulpit," 27
  crucified *pueblo*, see "*Pueblo*"
  removal of poor from (Sobrino), 32
Creatio ex nihilo, 87, 122
Creation, ix, xiii, 42, 44, 47–48, 52, 54–55, 63, 83, 88, 92–93, 116, 118, 122, 127–35

D
Desert between Mexico and United States, 28–29, 102–3
Deus absconditus, 7, 29, 32, 60, 65, 141
Deus crucifixus, 7, 32
Discernment, 18, 25–26, 61, 64, 87–90, 127
Disciplina arcani, 16–20, 26, 77–78
Dixit Dominus, 51
Dominant community, 18, 19, 29, 31, 67, 71–73, 94, 99, 103, 105, 106, 107, 114, 115
Dominican friars of *Quisquella*, 22–23, 104–6
Dualism(s), 10, 36–44, 46, 89, 128–30, 138

Subject Index

E
"*Ecclesia ab Abel*," 66
Ecclesiology, 4, 12–13, 52, 63, 66, 90, 105, 117, 131
Ecclesiophany, 66
Ecofeminism, 76, 109, 128–30
Epiclesis, 23, 94
Ethics
    and praxis, 115–16
    Bonhoeffer, 25, 91, 116, 149
Eucharist, 6, 12, 39, 46–48, 58, 61–65, 77, 80, 101, 111, 135
Evangelii Gaudium, 69, 94, 109, 110
Exitus et reditus, 63

F
Fathers and Mothers, Patristics and Matristics, xi–xii, 5, 8, 10, 11, 32, 41, 43, 47, 52, 57, 60, 67, 70, 89, 90, 109, 120
Fiesta, 27
"Fifth Mark" of the Church, see also "Solidarity with the poor," 108–9
Formation, *conformitas*, 23, 25–26, 91, 94–96, 113–14, 134–35
Fundamentalism, 37–38

G
Gaia, 131–32
Gemeinde, 6, 12, 13
Gestalt Christi, 13–16, 18–19, 22–24, 26–27, 29
Gnostic, Gnosticism, 16, 39
Grace, x, xv, 37, 46, 53, 54, 55, 62, 67, 70, 85, 138
    "cheap," 17
"Great Commission," The, 124

H
Heteronomy, 138
Holy Spirit, ix–x, 1, 3, 4, 5, 7, 8, 10, 12, 14, 17, 23–26, 34–35, 40–41, 43, 48, 57–59, 61, 62, 64–66, 67, 69–75, 77, 78, 87–96, 104, 106–7, 108, 111, 113, 115, 117, 118, 122–24, 126, 127, 135, 138, 141–42
    Comforter, ix
    Creator, 122–24
    "forgotten Person," 88–89
    obstruction of the Holy Spirit, 88
    Pater pauperum, 96
    soul of the Church, 124
    voice of the Preaching Church, ix, 71, 87–96, 135
Holy Spirit Parish, Kent, WA, 19, 100, 103
Holy Trinity, 8, 10, 40, 42–44, 55, 108, 118–26
    community and, 1, 62–63, 70, 118, 121–22, 124
    contemplation of, 10, 52, 53, 57, 60–61, 70, 89, 118–19, 121
    creation and, 92–93
    economic, 124–25, 141–42
    icon of the Church community, 63, 67, 70, 119–20, 124, 126, 141
    immanent, 124
    inclusive ways of speaking of, 92–93
    light of, 1, 7, 8, 122–23
    liturgy and, 62–65
    "New paradigm" of, 118–19
    perichoeresis and, 43, 52–54, 124, 127, 130, 135, 141–42
    relationship among Persons, 122–25
    two hands of God, 87–92, 124–26, 135
Homily, homiletic(s), 2, 6, 13, 52, 60, 61, 109–10
    "paying attention," 60–67, 88, 93
Human, humanity, xi, 3, 4, 9, 41, 47, 53, 62, 63–64, 82, 97, 116, 118, 120, 127, 129, 131, 132, 133, 140–41

Subject Index

Human, humanity *(continued)*
   dignity, 18–19, 34, 99, 101, 102, 130
   formation, 134–35
   of Christ, 6, 14–15, 21–22, 26, 32, 41–43, 44, 87
   responsibility, 83

I
Identity, 71–72, 78
   baptismal, 70
   Christian, 3, 15
   divine, 81
   with person of Christ, 21
"Illegal alien" (as inappropriate), see also "undocumented" and "migrant," 19, 99
Imago Dei, 41, 70
Immigration reform, 19, 100–101, 105, 135
In persona Christi, 64
"*Incarnatio continuo*," 65
Indigenous community and culture, see also "theology," x, 24, 40, 54, 111–13, 133
"*Ipse Christus*," 65

J
Jesus Christ
   Bridge, 41–44
   "Christ existing as Church community" (*Christus als Gemeinde existierend*), 13–14, 44, 49, 91, 104, 107
   Christology, 40–41, 63–64, 131
   "Christophany," 42, 59, 63–65, 116
   Hope Embodied, 32, 34
   Incarnation, 6, 14, 32, 33, 34, 40, 42, 64, 80, 88
   Mediator, 41
   "midpoint" in preaching (Fant), 7, 13–14, 19
   Nepantla of God, 40–41, 43–44, 51, 63

   poor as sacramental presence of, x, 4, 7, 10
   risen, 4, 7
   Sacrament, x, 39–41, 44, 45, 48, 50, 87
   Sacramental Word of the God of the Poor, 63, 87, 142
   Word, ix, x, 6, 7, 8, 10, 14 – 15, 39, 40 – 41, 44, 45, 48 – 49, 53 – 55, 63, 81, 87, 94, 104, 126, 141

K
Kenosis, 41, 65
Kerygma, 70, 78

L
Lampedusa, 101
Laudato Si, 83– 84, 109
Liturgy, 6, 17, 23, 58, 61–62, 64–65, 77, 110
Lumen Gentium, 69

M
Marks of the Church, 108–9
Martyr, martyrdom, 16–17, 26, 28, 32, 107, 126
Medellín, see also "CELAM," "Puebla," 109, 113
Medical Mission Sisters, 91
"Metaphor of the window" (Panikkar), 138
Metaphysics, 17, 37, 47, 81, 116, 129–30
Mexican immigrant community, see also "Preaching," xiv, 4, 5, 13, 15, 19, 23, 24, 27–29, 71–72, 99–107, 135
Migrant, biblical migrant (*ger*), 4, 99–100, 103
Modalism, 92, 121
Mother Earth (*Pacha Mama*), 33, 50, 78, 127–35
"Mug and jug" methodology, 111–12

Subject Index

"Mutual, communal, and reciprocal" (Boff), see also "new paradigm," 111–17
Mysticism, 89

N
Nazi era in Germany, 11, 17, 31, 53, 64, 105, 107, 125
Neo-liberalism, 36, 102
Neo-Platonism, 138
"New Age," 38
"New Homiletic," 2–3
"New paradigm," 132, 134
  preaching, 10, 111, 117
  sacramental, 45–46, 48, 114–15
  theological, 50, 111
  Trinitarian, 118–19
Nostra Aetate, 137

O
"Ontonomy," 137–42
"Opium of the people" (religion as), 26
Option for the poor, ix, 66–67, 72, 130
Our Father, The, 76–86
  and baptism, 78
  and the Beatitudes, 84
  and the divine name, 81
  and the Holy Spirit, 78
  all teachings of Jesus in, 77
  communal use of, 77, 78, 80, 81–82, 85, 86
  "Pearl of great price," 77
  prayer of the disciple, 76, 84
  prayer of solidarity with the cosmos, 77, 78
  prayer of solidarity with the poor, 78–79, 80
  reign of God as "very heart of the Lord's Prayer" (Boff), 82

P
Perichoeresis, see "Holy Trinity"
Poor, ix–x, 4, 5, 7–8, 10, 13, 15, 18, 26–28, 30, 31–35, 38, 40–41, 44, 49–50, 52–54, 55, 58, 61–63, 66, 68–69, 71–75, 78–81, 83–86, 88–91, 94–98, 102–4, 106–9, 111–15, 117, 119–21, 126–28, 130–35, 142
Posada, 103–4
Praxis
  and ethics, 116
  of discipleship, 4, 58, 97–98, 138, 140
  of justice, 104, 124
  of God, 81, 142
  of the poor, 58, 114–15, 141
  of preaching, 3, 41, 71, 82, 117
  orthopraxis, 109, 117
Prayer, 18, 47, 48, 53–55, 57–67, 68, 75, 76–86, 88, 91–96, 99–104, 106, 110, 123, 125, 141
Preaching, Preacher, ix, x, xii, 2–8, 10, 11–19, 22–24, 26, 27, 28, 31–35, 39, 40, 49, 51, 52, 53, 55, 57, 58, 62, 64, 65, 67, 69, 70, 71, 74, 78, 82, 88, 91, 93–98, 104–7, 109–12, 125–27, 134, 138, 140, 141, 142
  as dialogue, 51–56
  as discipline, 18
  as subversive action, 125–26
  crisis of, 2, 4, 39, 51, 110–11, 125
  incarnational preaching, 14
  Holy Preaching, x, 2, 3, 6, 8, 10, 11, 12, 15, 18, 20, 23, 30, 31, 32, 35, 39, 40, 41, 43, 44, 50, 51–55, 57–63, 65, 66, 67, 70, 71, 72, 74, 75, 78, 79, 84, 85, 86, 88–98, 104, 106, 110, 111, 113, 117, 119, 125, 126, 135, 138–42
  liturgy and, 2, 6, 17, 23, 61–62, 64–65, 88, 89, 110, 111
  praedicatio crucis, 31–35
  preacher as "resident theologian," 12

159

Subject Index

Preaching, Preacher *(continued)*
  preaching center, 142
  preaching event, 6, 7, 55, 61, 62, 97
  preaching methodology, 113
  Sunday preaching, x, 2, 4, 6, 11, 19, 23, 35, 39, 51, 55, 58, 62, 65, 71, 74, 93, 94–95, 97–98, 105, 109–11, 125
  theology of, xiii, xiv, xv, 10, 11, 12, 13, 20, 39, 54, 61, 62, 63, 109, 138, 139, 140
  "Who" of, 4, 6, 8, 10, 18, 24, 28, 57, 68–75, 79, 94, 140
  Puebla, see also "*CELAM*," "*Medellín*," 109, 113
Pueblo, ix–x, 10
  crucified *Pueblo*, 34–35
  icon of the Holy Trinity, 119, 121
  preaching *Pueblo*, 12–15, 18–19, 22–24, 26–30, 60, 65, 74, 91, 106–7, 142
  pueblo as community, 97
Pueblos jóvenes, 5, 84

Q
Quisquella (*La Española*), 22, 53, 104

R
Racism, 19
Ratio, 9–10
Real Presence, 39, 46–50, 61–65
Reign (Kingdom) of God, 2, 4, 34, 47, 48, 50, 55, 66, 76–80, 82, 113, 120
Relativism, 37
Rhetoric (homiletic), 3, 8, 39–40, 70, 126, 138
Roman Empire, 17, 36, 107

S
Sacra praedicatio, 6–7, 10, 15, 31–32, 56, 97, 107, 111, 135

Sacrament(s), 10, 12, 16, 39, 40, 44, 45–50, 62–63, 65, 71, 95, 104, 106, 114
  Baltimore Catechism definition, 46
  Christ as, see "Jesus Christ"
  Church as, see "Church"
  ex opere operantis, 46
  ex opere operato, 46, 73
  magical view of, 73–74
  Mysteries, 16, 17
  sacramentals, 48
  sacramentum mundi, 45–50, 114
Sacrosanctum Concilium, 48
Salus mundi, 34
Second Vatican Council, 2, 5, 45, 47–48, 64–65, 69, 101, 109, 110, 113, 114, 119, 137
Sendero Luminoso, 127
Silence, silent listening, 17, 53–55, 139–41
Sin(s), sinfulness, 14, 34, 35, 37, 38, 41, 43, 73, 83–86, 108, 130, 132
Solidarity (with the poor), ix, x, 28, 33, 35, 40, 44, 69, 72, 78, 86, 95 – 96, 100, 106, 107, 115, 120
  communal, 128, 135
  cosmic, 134
  "fifth mark" of the Church, 108–9
Southwestern United States, Mexican presence in, 102
Stations on the Way to Freedom (Bonhoeffer), 16–30, 31
Suffering Servant, 35, 123
Synergy, 5, 43, 111, 125

T
Table fellowship, 90
Taíno people, 22, 53, 104–6
"tempiternity," xiii
Theologoumenon (of Rahner), 124

Subject Index

Theology, xii, 3, 9–10, 38, 41, 60, 82, 96, 110, 111, 115, 116, 120, 121, 124, 128, 137
 and creation, 127–35
 as contemplation of the Holy Trinity, see "Holy Trinity"
 contextual, 11, 12, 15, 17, 27, 31, 32, 58, 64, 67, 105–6, 109, 113, 116, 119
 cosmic, xi
 Dominican, 15
 ecclesiology, 12, 52, 117
 Eastern Orthodox, 90
 ecofeminism, 67, 109, 128–30
 European, 37
 fundamental, 95
 historical, 105
 indigenous, 67, 109
 Latin American, 34, 67, 81, 116
 locus theologicus, loci theologici, 60–67
 of Bonhoeffer, 11–30, 105
 of the cross (*theologia crucis*), 7, 16, 27–28, 31–35
 of liberation, 3, 4, 61, 67, 109, 131, 133
 of preaching, xiii, xiv, xv, 4, 6, 10, 39–40, 52, 54, 61–63, 70, 109, 137–42
 Pneumatology, 59, 87–96
 sacramental, 45–50, 73, 90
 symbolic, 89
 systematic, 89
Theodicy, 83
Transecclesiation, 49, 64
Transfigured One, Transfiguration, 8, 52, 148
Transfinalization, 47
Transpauperation, 49
Transsignification, 47
Transubstantiation, 47
Transuniversation, 49
Transverbation, 7, 49
Tritheism, 121

U
Undocumented immigrant, 18, 29, 100, 103, 106
Unidad dual ("dual unity"), 40, 41, 44
Universe, see also "Cosmos," "Creation," ix, 33, 49, 50, 61, 62, 63, 65, 66, 127–35

V
Veni Creator Spiritus, 87, 92, 122
Veni Sancte Spiritus, 96
Via negativa, 121
"Vicarious representative action" (*Stellvertretung*), 21–31
Vicarius Christi, 24

W
Western thought, 36–38, 52, 64, 66, 132, 133
Women
 dignity of, 54, 90, 110, 128
 first Dominicans, 6, 62, 97, 111
 martyrs, xi – xii, 32
 "new way of doing theology," 129–30
Word (Scripture), ix–x, 2, 3, 14–15, 37, 39, 47–49, 54, 58, 61–65, 69, 73, 76, 81, 82, 89, 91, 92, 94–95, 99, 100, 106, 110, 111, 115, 117, 122, 134, 139–42

X
Xenophobia, 19

Scripture Index

Genesis

1:2	87, 122
1:3	122
1:27	41
17:16	54

Exodus

3:7	54
3:14	81
9:1	100
22:22–23	54

Leviticus

19:33–34	99

Numbers

11:25–29	123

Deuteronomy

10:18	54

Judges

3:10	123
6:34	123
11:29	123
13:24	123
14:6, 19	123
15:14	123

First Samuel

10:6	123
11:6	123
16:13	123
16:14	123

First Kings

19:11–13	x

Second Chronicles

15:1	123
20:14	123

Job

33:4	123

Psalms

34	58, 69
34:17	54
42	95
51:11	123
69:33	54
104:30	123
118:23	x
139:7	123
143:10	123

Scripture Index

Wisdom

18:14–15	139

Isaiah

11:2	123
30:1	123
32:15	123
34:16	123
40:9	32
40:13	123
42:1	123
44:3	123
48:16	123
53:4	123
59:21	123
61:1	123
63:10, 11, 14	123

Jeremiah

7:6	54

Ezekiel

2:2	123
3:12, 14, 24	123
8:3	123
11:1, 5, 24	123
36:26–27	123
39:29	123
43:5	123

Joel

2:28–29	123

Micah

3:8	123

Zechariah

4:6	123
7:10	54

Matthew

5:14	66
5:44	33
5:48	84
6:9–13	79
7:6	16
8:20	63
11:15	54
13:9	54
15:26	16
16:24	33
25	41, 100
25:31–40	99
25:31–46	54
25:40	49
28:19	124

Mark

1:12	59
4:9	54
7:27	16
11:23	74
16:15	ix

Luke

1:15, 35, 41, 67	123
2:25–27	123
3:16, 22	123
4:1, 14, 18	123
4:18–21	117
10:21	123
10:27	100
11:2	78
11:2–4	79
11:13	123
12:10, 12	123
16:19–31	67, 72

John

1:14	87
1:23	22
1:31, 3:5	123
3:8	88, 123

Scripture Index

3:16	45, 92	**Galatians**	
3:34	123	2:19–20	91
4:23	123	3:28	70
6:63	123		
7:39	123	**Ephesians**	
10:10	19, 33, 40, 80	1:23	65
14:17, 26	123	5:9	26
15:26	123		
16:13	123	**Philippians**	
17:3	95	2:5–11	41, 65
20:22	123		

Acts

First Thessalonians

2:1–13	124	5:17	57
17:28	125		

Romans

First Peter

5:20	70	1:6–7	26
8:19, 22–23	127	2:5	69
8:26	ix	2:9	1
8:26–27	58, 75	3:20–22	1
12:2	26		

First Corinthians

Revelation

12:27	43, 49	3:22	54
		5:8–10	2

www.ingramcontent.com/pod-product-compliance
Lightning Source LLC
Chambersburg PA
CBHW051932160426
43198CB00012B/2123